THE OBERON BOOK OF
MODERN MONOLOGUES FOR WOMEN
VOLUME 2

THE OBERON BOOK OF MODERN MONOLOGUES FOR WOMEN

Chosen and Edited by Catherine Weate

OBERON BOOKS
LONDON
www.oberonbooks.com

First published in 2013 by Oberon Books Ltd
521 Caledonian Road, London N7 9RH
Tel: 020 7607 3637 / Fax: 020 7607 3629
e-mail: info@oberonbooks.com
www.oberonbooks.com

A catalogue record for this book is available from the British Library.

PB ISBN: 978-1-84943-452-2
E ISBN: 978-1-84943-621-2

Cover image © mattonimages.co.uk

Printed, bound and converted
by CPI Group (UK) Ltd, Croydon, CR0 4YY.

Visit www.oberonbooks.com to read more about all our books and to
buy them. You will also find features, author interviews and news of any
author events, and you can sign up for e-newsletters so that you're always
first to hear about our new releases.

Catherine Weate is a freelance voice and dialect coach. She has worked in theatre, film, television, radio, education, commerce, law and politics across England, Australia, Hong Kong, Africa and India. Her former roles include: Head of Voice at Rose Bruford College, Head of Voice and Vice Principal at the Academy of Live and Recorded Arts and Head of Examinations at LAMDA. Catherine's other titles published by Oberon Books are: *Modern Voice: Working with Actors on Contemporary Text*, *Classic Voice: Working with Actors on Vocal Style*, *The Oberon Book of Modern Monologues for Women 1*, *The Oberon Book of Modern Monologues for Men 1*, *The Oberon Book of Modern Monologues for Men 2* and *The Oberon Book of Modern Duologues*.

INTRODUCTION

Monologues are an essential part of every actor's toolkit. Why? Because actors are required to perform monologues regularly throughout their career: in particular, preparing for drama school entry, showcasing skills for agents or auditioning for a professional role. But what actually is a monologue? And how do you go about choosing the right one for you?

A monologue is nothing more than a speech by a single character in a play or screenplay. Sometimes the character might speak their thoughts aloud to themselves, sometimes they might engage in a lengthy speech to another character and sometimes they will directly address the audience, breaking down the 'fourth wall'.

Choosing a monologue, however, is a delicate task. The only givens are that the character should be close to your age (or in your playing range) and the text should be sufficiently interesting (on its own without the rest of the play) to hold the attention of an audience. Most importantly, it must speak to you, resonate with your inner emotions, affect your senses, make you laugh or cry and draw you into a world that you want to hear more about. But don't forget that if you are using the monologue in a professional audition then it must resemble the job in some way, through genre, period, culture and/or character (including accent).

Some coaches have particular 'rules' for choosing a monologue. Let me assure you that there is no 'right' or 'wrong'. Trust your inner instincts when making your choice, as long as the piece is appropriate for the context in which it is to be performed. There are coaches who advise avoiding monologues that are: physically still, tell a story about the past, directly address the audience or use vulgarity. None of these rules apply (unless stipulated by an audition panel or casting agent). Controversial content is tricky to avoid in contemporary theatre texts (after all, modern plays often seek to mirror the real world), and a well-written character-driven story spoken directly to an audience can be riveting.

Other coaches advise actors to avoid monologue books; however, they can be a terrifically useful tool and a great starting point. Better than being overwhelmed by rows of plays in bookshops or libraries. They only work though if you read the full play text from which your monologue has been drawn. Picking a piece from a book and performing it without further reading or research is madness and, ultimately, your character study will be superficial and incomplete. Read the play to understand the journey/trajectory of plot, character, relationship and situation. If possible, try to see the play in performance to understand how the monologue (and therefore the character) works in context.

This monologue book showcases the writing from authors published by Oberon Books (following on from the first volume of *The Oberon Book of Modern Monologues for Women*, published in 2008). There are a diverse range of quirky and memorable characters that cross cultural and historical boundaries. Yes, some of them tell stories, many directly address the audience and, being contemporary plays, there is quite a bit of controversial material. As there should be.

The pieces have been organised into age-specific groups: 'teens', 'twenties', 'thirties' and 'forties plus'. However, there is the occasional character that crosses these boundaries so do spend some time reading outside of your age-related box just in case. The boundaries are simply there to provide you with a starting point.

Monologue length varies widely depending on the material: the concise and contained to the weighty and protracted. Don't be afraid of adapting them to your needs, particularly when many auditions stipulate time frames for performance. In a few cases I have cut texts to maintain flow and sense. This is indicated by '…' on a line all of its own, between paragraphs.

If you require any further information or advice on these books (all feedback is welcome) or in choosing/performing a monologue then please contact me through my website (www.catherineweate.com) or on twitter (@voicesupport). In the meantime, happy reading.

Catherine Weate

CONTENTS

PART ONE: TEENS

PART TWO: TWENTIES

PART THREE: THIRTIES

PART FOUR: FORTIES PLUS

PART ONE: TEENS

.

BLACKBERRY TROUT FACE
by Laurence Wilson

*This play was first performed at the Unity Theatre, Liverpool
on 29 September 2009.*

Set in Liverpool, *Blackberry Trout Face* explores the lives of
three teenagers who are struggling to cope on their own. Jakey
(18), KERRIE (15) and Cameron (13) have been abandoned
by their mother, a heroin addict who feeds her habit through
prostitution. KERRIE receives a text from her and, thinking
she knows where she is, leaves in the middle of the night. She
returns in the morning, alone, drenched and dejected. In the
following scene, she explains what happened to Jakey and
Cameron.

KERRIE

She sent me a text. It said, I'm at a special place. So I thought I knew where she was. There's this park right near the river, where yer can see the Runcorn Bridge. I've been there with me Mum a few times. We'd sit off and look at it and I'd tell her all the stuff I knew about it, while we had a flask of tea and some cookies. We called it our special place. *(Beat.)* So I thought she had to be there.

It was freezin but I didn't care coz I knew she was gonna be there, waitin for me. I kept thinking, she'll hug away the cold.

…

It was still dark when I got there. The bridge was all lit up though and it was all reflectin in the water and it looked dead beautiful.

…

She wasn't there. So I texted her and waited.

…

I waited for a reply.

…

But the special place she was at, wasn't our special place.

…

I kept textin her and textin her, telling her where I was; to come and get me, until I had none left. Then the sun come up and the bridge wasn't beautiful anymore. Just a bridge. Ugly, cold metal. *(Beat.)* Then finally she texted me back.

…

She said she's with some old friends from years ago, on the South Coast and that they're overlookin some river. She said there's this really nice little bridge goin across it and that it reminds her of me. A special place. She said she'll tell me about it one day when she sees me. Oh yeah and er… Keep safe.

APPLES
by John Retallack

Apples *was first performed at The Empire, Middlesbrough on 2 June 2010.*

This monologue is entitled 'CLAIRE'S SOLUTION'. CLAIRE is 15 years old and was raped at a party by a boy from school after she had passed out from a cocktail of alcohol and drugs. She became pregnant and now has a baby boy, whom she isn't able to name. Her life has been turned upside down by the baby and she is no longer able to go out with her friends or even get Gary's attention: she still feels some connection to him despite the rape. CLAIRE has heard that her friend Eve recently slept with Gary but, in fact, Gary raped Eve as well. Eve and Debbie are on holiday in Majorca and CLAIRE feels jealous and resentful of her friends. It seems the only way out is to get rid of the baby. She speaks directly to the audience, except for the line in speech marks.

CLAIRE

We cried into each other's faces
at least there was no one around to see me bawling
Five minutes later we reached the beck again
we stood at the side of the bridge
The water rose and surged like a black brick road

I thought of Eve and Debbie in Majorca
sunning themselves
not giving a care about the people back home
I imagined them banging a bunch of Spanish hunks

I was fucking jealous
Eve probably didn't even care about Gary
she had that special way of using people
and getting whatever she wanted

To baby boy

'What are we gonna do with you?'

He didn't seem to know
His tantrums started all over again
the noise was incredible

What an ugly idiot he was

My brain was overflowing with babies, boys and bitches
it fucking knacked

I told Eve it was Gary's baby
she still went and shagged him

I cuddled the little knobhead in my arms for a minute

The crying was unbearable
I really wanted to strangle it
It struck me for the rest of my life

I'd only have the Baby Boy for company

so far he hadn't been much of a mate

I stood him on top of the bridge railing
we had a dance as the wind eased up a bit
I made a little prayer
scrunched my eyes
and accidentally on purpose threw him off the rail

There was a big plop in the water
and a bit of red where he must've smacked off the bottom

I faked a look of horror

Gary's jaw and my hair colour and cheekbones
washing down the dirty stream

I felt a bit sick, but at least I'd got it over with
I pushed my lips together and charged down the road again
the breeze still going but nothing holding me back

I felt like all the estate's eyes were on me
but killing the baby was just a silly mistake
We've all been there
When I got in
I made sure to phone 999 straight away
I waited for them to come round
I had a story in my head
I stared at the windows

I felt alright
The sky wasn't exactly glowing but all the black clouds
they were diamonds

BUD TAKE THE WHEEL, I FEEL A SONG COMING ON

by Clara Brennan

This play was first performed at The Underbelly, on 5 August 2010, as part of the Edinburgh Fringe Festival, produced by Reclaim Productions and SPL.

FRANCES is a troubled sixteen-year-old who lives with her family in an old mill town, deep in the English countryside. She is pregnant to Liam (in his early thirties) who is apprenticed to her father, the local thatcher. FRANCES' brother, Christian (in his late twenties), has returned after an eight-year absence hoping to develop the old mill for the company he works for. It has been a painful journey back as their father beat him savagely as a child. FRANCES has not exchanged a single word with her father since her brother left. In this monologue, FRANCES tries to bring Christian up-to-date with her life – at least, superficially. She begins by explaining the terms 'Epic Win' and 'Epic Fail'.

FRANCES

Like – last summer I went to an 'Epic Win' party in a field
out by White Farm with my mates. We camped. Some of
them had just gotten back from this trip to Barcelona, my art
teacher organised it. But I couldn't go – which was an Epic
Fail. I'm the only one that even had a job – shampoos and sets
at fucking *Snips*, that lame-ass hairdressers next to Abbey
National? I fucking *hated* it and I still didn't have enough to
go, pay for the bed and board and the flights. But I was the
only one who knew who Antoni Gaudi was. I mean, Christie,
that school's still a fucking shit-hole! You know the director
of the Architecture College Gaudi went to, said once: 'I don't
know if we've given the degree to a genius or to a lunatic.
Time will give the answer.' I thought that was brilliant, you
know – half my teachers hate me and half of them think
the sun like, shines out of my arse. You were the same, I
remember. So in 1926, he, Gaudi, goes for a little walkabout
like all days, and gets run over by a streetcar. He had no ID
on him, and his clothes were old, the poor sod looked like a
tramp, and so they took him to a hospital for poor people.
Finally, at the very last minute, a priest recognized him. They
always do, don't they. Three days after, he died. A genius or a
lunatic. Epic.

Ha, and my mate Georgina, I don't think we were friends
when you were at home we only met at Secondary, she saw
a photo of his Sagrada Familia and thought she was going to
fucking Disney Land! Disney Land, that's just genius, isn't
it?! Anyway, my mates all come back saying how they'd had
the most amazing time, like, ever? And how they'd gotten

pissed with Mr Holdsworth, my art teacher, the one who's obsessed with Bonnard's wife in the bath? Anyway, they'd drunk sangria, and then this authentic Spanish thing, which is red wine mixed with coca-cola. So that's what we were drinking last summer in a field full of crispy-coated cowpats. The usual glamour. We had a fire, there were guitars, we got wasted. I lost my virginity to my friend Dave. Yeah, Little Dave. But he's my mate, it wasn't anything. He can play The Beatles catalogue by ear. We sang the whole of *Rubber Soul.* We shared a tent. It was, curiosity. I mean, we were just kids. And the big surprise is – the incredible thing is – Dave didn't tell anyone. And neither did I until now. And that's weird for teenagers. It is. Believe me.

SENSE

by Anja Hilling
(translated by Logan Kennedy
and Leonhard Unglaub)

from *Theatre Café: Plays Two*

*Sense was first performed in the UK on 27 April 2009
(as part of Theatre Café) at Southwark Playhouse, London.*

Sense follows the lives of a group of teenagers and their search for friendship, love and identity. Their experiences are separated into I. Eyes, II. Nose, III. Skin, IV. Ears and V. Tongue. PHÖBE's story is part of I. Eyes. She meets Fred, who is blind, at an eighteenth birthday party and is drawn into his world. He asks her to go swimming at the lake and, on the way, she becomes obsessed with his eyes and how he must 'see' the world.

PHÖBE

Lost myself in his eyes for more than forty minutes. And it wasn't like looking into anyone else's eyes. It was different. It was one-way. No back and forth. No exchange. Nothing came back at me. And I didn't notice a single one of the stops the train made. I'm not lying that's the way it was. I was inside his eye-sockets. Disappeared into them for forty minutes. I didn't see anything there or else I forgot everything. I haven't the faintest clue what goes on in there. But I was there. Happily. And then full of rage. I find you excessive in your blindness. Unreachable exaggerated an overdose. Awful. Helpless and unspeakably elegant. I see you beneath the stars zipping headlong through a universe. Then tripping over the curb. Your hand that always misses. Your hand in my bloodstream. Your foot in the gap between train and platform. I see you stumbling through the night. Falling over stones on the way to the lake. Gliding through the Milky Way. I want to be close to you. Closer.

I want to know how much more there is.

Behind your eyes.

I have a thousand questions.

Is it bright or dark your world.

Does music move inside you.

Like a snake maybe or like a spider or something.

Do noises have a smell and what about me.

Can you smell me.

Am I a colour a sound a movement.

Am I three-dimensional.

What do you think when you hear my voice.

Do you imagine me. Have an image.
Where would it come from.
Do you even know what that is. An image.
Or is there just a desert inside you.
Where nothing can grow.
I really want to know that want to see that.
The landscape behind your eyes.
I want to see what you see.
See myself with your eyes.
Whiz through your eyeballs.
Explode into your universe.
Be inside you shine and scream.
…
Then I blacked out.

SENSE

by Anja Hilling
(translated by Logan Kennedy
and Leonhard Unglaub)

from *Theatre Café: Plays Two*

Sense was first performed in the UK on the 27 April 2009 (as part of Theatre Café) at Southwark Playhouse, London.

Sense follows the lives of a group of teenagers and their search for friendship, love and identity. Their experiences are separated into I. Eyes, II. Nose, III. Skin, IV. Ears and V. Tongue. NATASCHA's story is part of V. Tongue. She hates hearing the noise of people speaking and avoids speaking herself. However, things change when she hears Albert call out to her by name at the local swimming pool.

NATASCHA

Natascha. Natascha.

A miserable word.

That's how it always starts.

Natascha.

After that nothing but night. Nothing.

That's what it's like my name.

A cruel beginning.

Three torturous syllables.

Three As. Three yelps of pain.

A T in the middle.

A beat a trembling t-t-t-t-t-t.

A pulsing in the auricle. A tensing in the brain muscles.

What follows I know it it's always the same always pain.

Words words words.

Questions little jokes words words.

What follows. I never understand it. Never.

A voice shoots into me.

Bursts my eardrum.

Shoots letters into my small head.

Tears down bridges between my organs.

Pressure on the eyes velvet on the tongue shortness of breath.

My brain bursts into flame my lips twitch.

Someone wants to talk to me wants to hear answers.

It often starts with my name.

I say nothing. I can't

It's not that I don't have an answer. I don't have a voice.

My answer is a scream.

Nobody hears it. I don't scream audibly.

I want to leave. As fast as I can.

I don't run.

I can't find the bridge to my legs.

I'm gushing in bloodstreams scream in soundproof chambers.

Then I smile.

When someone says my name I smile.

When everything inside me turns to night my face smiles.

My smile is a free spirit.

I know it's strange.

Smiling doesn't fulfil the expectations doesn't count as an answer.

Smiling is always too little. Or too much.

…

When Albert says my name there's no smile in me. Only music.

I know who he is.

Student rep Albert. Hero of class contributors.

But the sound of his voice has the power to carry me.

With three syllables across the kiddy pool.

I'm afraid.

It's a new fear.

I'm afraid he might go without saying another word.

SHRADDHA
(Faith: You are what's in your heart)
by Natasha Langridge

Shraddha *was first performed at Soho Theatre, London, on 29 October 2009.*

The Romany Gypsies are about to be evicted from the building site of the London Olympics. Understandably they are more suspicious than usual of outsiders (gorgers). PEARL PENFOLD is 17 years old and has been promised in marriage to another Romany community. However, she and Joe, a gorger from the local council estate have fallen in love. They run away together and PEARL tells fortunes at a local festival so they can eat. Joe asks her what she tells her customers and PEARL replies…

PEARL

I say, 'Give me ye palm dearie' then

'Oh dordy

Ye've had a difficult time haven't ye dear

Life's been hard on ye hasn't it?

And she give me

her bracelet to read

'But ye gonna have a long life

And

Oh

What's this?

Oh yes

And ye do deserve it don't ye dear

A beautiful house and what a garden and

There be

Oh

There is someone ye've to BEWARE of

DANGER

Who is it?

Can't quite see

Getting a bit hazy

If ye could just see ye way te give me a little more I might be
able to see clearly dear'

And she says she can give me a fiver but don't have no change and
I say that's alright dear and I take the tenner what's in her hand
and she say, 'Thank you'

…

'Now,' I say, 'Does ye know a woman with a name beginning with

A, B, C, or D?'
And she look even blanker than before in her eyes so I say 'Is it
D E F or G is it?
I think it might be an H?'
Her eyes light up a bit
So I says 'H yes BEWARE a woman whose name begins with H'

And she say, 'I knew
I knew I couldn't trust her'

And then it took me over. Like it were doing it on its own

'But it don't matter dear, cos that special someone, ye haven't met
him yet but if ye keep ye eyes open for a lovely man he's wearing
them brown Wellington things, black jeans with a rip over the right
thigh, a green t-shirt an there's a thin bit of cotton or something
round his neck and he's got a speck of brown in his blue eyes.
His hair is blond he's pushing it back with his hand.
He will love ye and lead ye onto the right path.
And that dear
is that – fer now
I tired out'

She yawns theatrically.

'I ain't got no more te give ye
Not even a bit o gold fer comfort
Cos ye know ye should never take gold from a Gypsy
But a Gypsy can take gold from ye and ye know it will bring ye
luck like ye never had and most important of all dear it will bring
ye protection'
And that were when she takes off this amulet from her bracelet
and place it down in front of me and say, 'Thank you very much'

DNA

by Dennis Kelly

DNA *was first performed in the Cottesloe Theatre of the National Theatre, London, on 16 February 2008.*

A group of teenagers bully, torture and kill (or so they think) one of their classmates. LEAH and Phil weren't involved but they are very much part of the same gang and Phil organises a bold cover-up. This monologue occurs before LEAH and Phil are told about the supposed killing. LEAH expresses her fears about the violent atmosphere in the school.

LEAH

A Field. LEAH and PHIL, PHIL eating an ice cream.

LEAH: What are you thinking?

No answer.

No, don't tell me, sorry, that's a stupid, that's such a stupid –

You can tell me, you know. You can talk to me. I won't judge you, whatever it is. Whatever you're, you know, I won't, I won't…

Is it me?

Not that I'm –

I mean it wouldn't matter if you weren't or were, actually, so –

Are you thinking about me?

No answer.

What good things? Phil? Or…

I mean is it a negative, are you thinking a negative thing about –

Not that I'm bothered. I'm not bothered, Phil, I'm not, it doesn't, I don't care. You know. I don't…

What, like I talk too much? Is that it? That I talk too much, you, sitting there in absolute silence thinking 'Leah talks too much, I wish she'd shut up once in a while' is that it, is that what you're, because don't, you know, judge, you know, because alright, I do. There, I'm admitting, I am admitting, I talk too much, so shoot me. So kill me, Phil, call the police, lock me up, rip out my teeth with a pair of rusty pliers, I talk too much, what a crime, what a sin, what an absolute catastrophe, stupid, evil, ridiculous, because you're not perfect actually, Phil. Okay? There. I've said it, you're not…

You're a bit…

You're…

Pause. She sits.

Do I disgust you? I do. No, I do. No don't because, it's alright, it's fine, I'm not gonna, you know, or whatever, you know it's not the collapse of my, because I do have, I could walk out of here, there are friends, I've got, I've got friends, I mean alright, I haven't got friends, not exactly, I haven't, but I could, if I wanted, if I wanted, given the right, given the perfect, you know, circumstances. So don't, because you haven't either, I mean it's not like you're, you know, Mr, you know, popular, you know, you haven't, you know, you haven't, you know, you haven't, but that's, that's different, isn't it, I mean it is, it is, don't say it isn't, really, don't, you'll just embarrass us both because it is different, it's different because it doesn't matter to you. Does it. Sitting there. Sitting there, all…

all…

You're not scared. Nothing scares, there, I've said it; scared. Scared, Phil. I'm scared, they scare me, this place, everyone, the fear, the fear that everyone here, and I'm not the only one, I'm not the only one, Phil, I'm just the only one saying it, the fear that everyone here lives in, the brutal terror, it scares me, okay, I've said it and I am not ashamed. Yes, I am ashamed but I'm not ashamed of my shame, Phil, give me that much credit at least, thank you.

Everyone's scared.

S'not just me.

Pause.

We've got each other.

We need each other.

So don't give it all…

You need me as much as…

Don't give it all the…

Beat.

What are you thinking?

THE WOMAN BEFORE
by Roland Schimmelpfennig,
translated by David Tushingham

The first performance of The Woman Before *took place at the Royal Court Jerwood Theatre Downstairs at Sloane Square, London on 12 May 2005.*

Teenagers, Andi and TINA are in love but Andi's family is moving away so they must separate. Here, TINA describes (for the audience) their last night together. Little do they know that Andi will be dead soon, killed by his father's ex-lover who turned up unexpectedly to reclaim a promise of undying love. After being rejected again, she makes love to Andi, kills him and packs him up into one of the moving boxes.

TINA

We meet as it's getting dark at the top of the bank like we always do, and then we go to the cinema.

The film tells the story of a woman who's got to find Pandora's Box before it falls into the hands of a man who's going to use it to threaten the whole world. The chase extends over several continents. It leads them from Greece to England and then on to Russia, China and finally Africa, the birthplace of humanity.

We follow our heroine in submarines, on motorbikes, in jeeps, by parachute, ship, on horseback, suspended from helicopters.

Then we get the bus home. It's half past eleven and we're back at the top of the bank again, outside. It's cold and I'm not dressed for it but it's still too early to go to mine. By half past twelve it's so cold I can't stand it any more and we go to mine.

I go in the front door, Andi waits down in the garden by my window.

Everything in the house is dark, everything's quiet, my parents are asleep upstairs, on the first floor.

My room's in the basement. Andi climbs in through the window not making a sound. Everything's quiet.

We lie side by side in my narrow bed in the dark in silence. No music. Above us and around us – like an ancient mausoleum – the house, a small bathroom, my room and the cellar downstairs, the kitchen and the living room on the ground floor, upstairs my parents' bedroom and a second bathroom.

Just as we are, naked, we start running through the house. Without making a sound we move through the rooms in the dark, along the hall, up and down the stairs. We stand still outside my parents' bedroom and then go on, out of the front door and into the garden, naked despite the cold, onto the lawn and then back downstairs again to my room.

Suddenly my dad's standing in the room in pyjama trousers and a top.

'Out, get out now – ' and he grabs hold of Andi and drags him, past my mother who's screaming, up the stairs and throws him out of the house.

I run back down the stairs, lock my door from the inside and climb out of the window with our things. My dad shouts after us.

On the way to his parents' Andi gets the pen out. We put our tag everywhere, on every wall, every drive, every garage door, his name and my name together. Andi and Tina together. The pen passes from him to me and back again. No and, no hearts, just our tag – exactly as we are, side by side, on everything all the way to his.

And then when we're outside the door he says: well then –

Brief pause.

I love you but we'll never see each other again. Yes, I say, I know. Take care. Goodbye.

NIGHTBLIND

by Darja Stocker
(translated by Philip Thorne)

from *Theatre Café: Plays Two*

Nightblind *was first performed in the UK in November 2008 (as part of Theatre Café) at the Unicorn Theatre, London.*

In *Nightblind*, LEYLA's life is falling apart and her story is told through a series of memory flashbacks. In this scene, she recalls (for the audience) finding the courage to end a poisonous relationship with BULL. However, he cannot accept her decision and reacts with violence.

LEYLA

It started off so well
When I tell him I want to leave the club
go out
talk with him
he agrees straight away

We sat on his bed
BULL and I
he even looked me in the eyes
when I said it

Silence
he'd seen it coming

I go to the door
he grabs hold of me
embraces me
tight
You don't want this
he says

Princess
I can see
you don't want this
you don't really want this
He says he loves me
He says I'm the one and only
He says he'll
hack me to shreds
if he has to
kill my mother

my brother
my father
set fire to our house
he says he loves me so much
that he'd have to kill himself
if I left him
This twitching mouth
this mad gleam in his eyes
I know what's coming
I want to get out the door
but my wrists
are cemented
in his grip
I head-butt his chin
feel his clenched fist
in my stomach
my breasts
in all the places
he normally strokes me
Doesn't look at me while he's doing this
Doesn't look at me
Doesn't look
Even when puke trickles from my mouth
and I scream like an animal
he still
doesn't
look

MUHAMMMAD ALI AND ME
by Mojisola Adebayo
from *Mojisola Adebayo: Plays One*

Muhammad Ali and Me *was created by the Ali Collective and first performed at the Oval House Theatre, London on 11 November 2008.*

Inspired by real-life experiences, *Muhammad Ali and Me* is the story of MOJITOLA, a young girl from Nigeria who grows up in England. Her father abandons her to a foster carer in South London at the age of five so that she can receive a 'good' education but she is sexually abused by the carer's son, Jimmy. MOJITOLA deals with her troubled life by retreating into her imagination, creating conversations with the American boxer Muhammad Ali. In this way, she learns to fight for her rights. When she starts studying A Level Law in her late teens, she finds the courage to walk into a police station and denounce her abusers.

MOJITOLA

I want to speak to a police officer *(POLICE OFFICER gestures to REFEREE.)* No. I want to report this to you.

…

This is nothing but the truth. It happened a long time ago. But I still dream about it, a lot, in the day. It plays… It makes me feel strange and a bit dirty, and angry. When I was less than five years old, my foster mother's grown-up son, Jimmy, sexually abused me. He made me touch him, when Angie went down the Elephant, Elephant and Castle shopping centre. He held it in his hand. I thought it was a trick with his thumb… It's like a tiny video that rewinds and plays again and again in my head. Everything else is blank. I don't remember anything else. Except maybe the dark circles on the carpet, the being afraid. Time I guess has erased the rest. Sometimes I shake and I freeze. It's like I'm on pause but everything else is still playing, moving forward. *(Becoming distressed.)* And I'm stuck in time. Frozen. I can't speak I can't move I can't *feel* I can't – it's like my body is a prison and I want to, I want to move, I want to be released, I want to scream, I want to be happy and I don't know how and I'm scared that I never will. *(A pause for calm.)* I know there's not enough evidence. I am doing A Level Law at the moment so… But I just wanted you to know. And I wanted to tell…you. Because it's a crime isn't it? You're not supposed to, to a child. *(Beat.)* And I'm gonna tell you something else. Cos I'm a witness, not a grass, and abuse is abuse: my dad used to hit my mum. Beat her up. Pound her like a punch bag. Or wrestle her. Slam her against the wall. Do you know how that sounds? Flesh on concrete block. Hearing her screams and me static, senseless, immobilised with shock. Yeah, body shots mostly, until the end. Cos left hooks, upper cuts, jabs – they show up. People ask questions. But I remember, a straight right to her face, because it's my first memory, the first time I froze. I was cuddled up next to her on the sofa watching the tele, then he came at her and it came through me. Smashing her glasses into her face. Blood running down her nose, dripping from her chin. It's criminal isn't it? Beyond reasonable doubt. I was two. She was, maybe twenty-two. I froze, for hours. She got away in the end. I understand. She's safe, somewhere. But I wanted you to know. I wanted to tell you. I want you to write it down. *(MOJITOLA points to POLICE OFFICER speaking forcefully, he could be her dad or…)* It's a crime! There are *rules. (MOJITOLA goes to leave, then changes her mind.)* And one more thing: you're supposed to look after your kids, Dads. You're not supposed to leave them. Forget them. Forget you had them. Not turn up when you're supposed to, on time. Forget birthdays you bastards. You're not supposed to leave them, to grow up Black, in Britain, alone with no one to show… *(Small pause.)* There's 99 names for God, in Islam. Not one of them *father.* How was I supposed to learn to be? When I can't even pronounce my own name.

PROTOZOA

by Kay Adshead

from *The Oikos Project*

This play was first performed at The Jellyfish Theatre in London on 23 September 2010.

Set in a not too distant future, *Protozoa* explores the experiences of survivors who were caught up in flooding that obliterated civilisation in England. This monologue occurs towards the beginning of the play during the course of a neighbourhood meeting. SHEANN is 18 and a black or mixed-race Northerner. She has lost her baby and wanders into the public building, naked, bleeding and in shock.

SHEANN

(Softly, very intimately, as if speaking to someone she knows.)

Well,
I've just come
from the
library,

and
my daughter
i'nt there.

There
was no-one
at the front
desk

no-one
at all,

not even
that ginger
minger
with the jumpers,

that won't
let you
eat crisps.

I went
up
the winding
staircase,

I've never
done that
before,

and there's
pictures
hanging on
the walls
in those
twiddly frames

of
really old
men,
important
men –
like off
the telly
sometimes,
with fuzzy
hair on
their face
and
watches on
chains.

I went
to the top,

and the door was open…

heavy
wood door

carved with

waves from

the sea

and great

smiley faced

fishes

with curly

tails

and

men in

boats

and I

went into

the room

which was

long

and dark

and dusty

with

piles of

broken books

from

floor to

ceiling

piles and piles.

And then

the moon
must have
come from
behind a
cloud,

I suppose
it did

I suppose
that's what
must have
happened,

and I
saw then

that the
room

was full
of
dead children…

and they
were
lying on
the floor

and their
eyes were
open and
staring,

and they'd

put the
little ones,
the babies,
together
in the far
corner

and I
had to
like
step through
being
really careful

Softer still.

And I'm sorry
I'm really sorry
but
I stepped
on a hand

I stepped
on a tiny
finger

I looked
and I looked

but my
baby,
my Sascha
wasn't there,

I'm sure of it,
I'm sure of it.

So

after a
while I
tip toed
back down
the staircase,

and I saw
that most
of the windows
had no
glass,

it had
shattered
and was
lying in
sparkly piles

and I

picked up
a long
sharp jagged
bit

and I
scratched out
the
eyes of

the painted
old men,

I scratched
them out.

LOVE STEALS US FROM LONELINESS
by Gary Owen

This play was commissioned and produced by the National Theatre Wales and its first performance was at Hobos, Bridgend on 7 October 2010.

Set in Bridgend in Wales, *Love Steals Us from Loneliness*, focuses on the family and friends of a teenager (Lee) killed in a car accident. CATRIN is Lee's girlfriend. It's Halloween and she has stormed out of the pub after an argument. Lee's best friend, Scott, follows her. CATRIN thinks Scott is gay and tells him that he should find a 'nice boy' like Lee. Here, she describes her first time with him. However, a little later, Scott confesses to CATRIN that he is in love with her.

CATRIN

…my first time I got like really panicky and my head was spinning and I was gonna chuck, and I thought if I try to stop him now, he's gonna go wild, he's just gonna you know hit me and it'll be like a rape thing and I can't hack that so I'm just gonna have to go through with it – and he stops.

He says, you alright?

I don't say nothing cos I'm like – on a knife edge.

He climbs off me, goes what's wrong?

Right then I gag. I clamp my hands over my mouth, not quite quick enough to stop the first wave of cider-vom spraying all over him.

And does he go wild? Does he fuck. He holds my hair, strokes my back while I'm chucking up into his mum's u-bend, and dabs the little strands of sick away from my mouth with pink quilted toilet paper. All this still with a huge hard-on poking out his boxers.

And I'm riding the spasms of puke, thinking – please God, please God, please don't let me wee myself in front of him – because that might be a step too far on a first date.

But then in between retches, I turn, and I look into his eyes – still watering red from the acid in my sick – and I realise, it's alright.

Lee's a really really decent bloke.

He'll accept me for who I am.

And I just – relax.

…

And he's fine with it. Puts my knickers and the bathroom mat
in the wash, lends me a pair of his pants.
Even says I look cute in them.
He's that lovely.
And that's what you want, for your first time. A nice boy.

SUZANNAH

by Jon Fosse
(translated by May-Brit Akerholt)

from *Jon Fosse: Plays Five*

The English-language version of Suzannah *was first performed by the Synergy Theatre Company in East Sussex in 2008.*

In *Suzannah*, the Norwegian playwright Jon Fosse gives voice to the wife of Henrik Ibsen, intertwining the stories of THE YOUNG SUZANNAH, The Middle-Aged Suzannah and The Old Suzannah. In this monologue, we hear how she first met Ibsen at her family home in Bergen and, despite the advice of her best friend, decided to marry him.

THE YOUNG SUZANNAH

And he

Henrik Ibsen

author and dramatist

and Artistic Director of The Norwegian Theatre

is invited to our home

Here

Today

Magdalene-stepmother asked him here

And the table is laid for three

for the three of us

Short pause

But Ibsen is so shy

quite short pause

and when I spoke to him

he looked down

and then quickly up

before he looked down again

Ibsen only looks down

And he says

almost nothing

And

giggles to herself

he walks past down on the street

She looks out of the window

And he looks up

And I wave to him

and now and then

yes he stops and he waits

and I go down to him

And we walk along the streets of Bergen

and we talk

About theatre

About the art of writing

And I've told my best friend

Karoline

I've told her

that he

that Ibsen

flings one arm out to the side

he's the one I want

…

And she

Karoline

mimics her

says do I really want him

Ibsen doesn't know how to behave

she says

and small

he's so small

And so unsure of himself

so clumsy

They laugh at him

In the theatre they laugh at Ibsen

she says

He doesn't look at the actors

not at the women

at least

when he directs

That's what she says

In a hassling tone

And then he walks around wearing those

yellow gloves

and makes a fool of himself in front of all of Bergen

Karoline says

Him

Do I really want him

him

she says

…

Yes I want Ibsen

him and no one else

I said to Karoline

Short pause

And now Ibsen's coming here

The table's laid for him

for me

And for Magdalene-stepmother

Short pause

And in only a few days

one

two

three

five

ten

I'm going to a ball

at The Philharmonic Society

And Ibsen's coming as well

And then it'll all be decided

Quite short pause

Because that's what I've decided

PART TWO:
TWENTIES

OPEN HEART SURGERY
by Laura Lomas

Open Heart Surgery *is part of* Theatre Uncut, *a compilation
of short plays written as a response to the British government's
spending cuts announced in 2010.* Theatre Uncut *was first
performed at the Southwark Playhouse in London on 16 March
2011. On 19 March, eighty-nine groups nationwide (with six
additional groups internationally) performed the plays as part
of a theatrical demonstration.*

In *Open Heart Surgery* we find a young woman, LISA, sitting
on a chair next to an empty hospital bed. She speaks directly
to the audience about her fiancé who has just had open heart
surgery. However, it soon becomes clear that he is an allegory
for the heart of a nation. LISA's final words are telling: 'But it
scares me, cus it's not the tearing up that's hard. Is it, when you
think about it? It's the putting back together.'

LISA

They'll be back soon. They said they would. They wanted to come sooner, but I asked if I could, you know. Just have 5 minutes, on our own. Two of us.

Talk to him.

Tell him stuff.

Just sit, for a bit.

She looks at the bed. She turns back to us. Plays with her necklace.

He gave me this, when we got engaged. Couldn't afford a ring, so he give me this till we get some money.

She shows us her pendant, it is half a heart.

He's got the other half. Wears it all the time, even though, you know, they're technically for girls. Lads at work take the piss. Said he dunt care. He's funny like that.

She looks at the bed.

He dunt look too bad I think, do you think? You know considering that… He could look worse. Could look a lot worse, but… Face is a bit pale, but that's just the blood, int it? It is. The nurse told me. Cus he's lost, he has lost quite a bit I think. But that's not bad, they said. Dunt mean nothing.

Beat. She looks at the bed.

He's sleeping now.

He'll be dreaming. You can tell he is cus the way his eyes are half open. He always sleeps like that. Used to think it was weird when we first met. Like he was watching me. I don't now, think it's sort of sweet. Sort of like he's half here, and half there, half with me even in his sleep.

I bet he's having a mad one. He always has mad dreams, always waking me to tell me them going 'Lisa! Guess what!' And I'm like 'I don't care Danny it's 5 in the morning.'

Stupid. Like a kid or something.

Said he dreamt he met Obama the other night. Said it was really nice. They were having a beer in the Swan.

I tried talking to him earlier, but I couldn't think of what to say. It's not that there isn't stuff, loads of stuff I want to…but I couldn't think how to say it. Make it make sense, when it doesn't. Does it? None of this doesn't even make any…

It's not just me that's feeling it. It's everyone. Nurse keeps coming in to check on us. Ask how I'm doing. She touched my shoulder when she left the room. I think she can feel it too, this sort of, sense of devastation.

Sort of leaks out, doesn't it?

Beat. She pauses, collects herself.

They've changed his bandages, and the bag at the bottom.

That's all the blood drainin' from his chest. It's the fifth one they've changed. I've been counting. Seems like a lot dunt it?

Seems like loads, but it's not. Just normal apparently. I asked her, the nurse and she said it's dead normal 'In a procedure like this, it's to be expected', she said.

But I don't know. I think it can't be good you know? To lose that much blood, can't be good for no one.

FANTA ORANGE
by Sally Woodcock

*The first performance of this play was at the
Finborough Theatre, London on 1 November 2011.*

REGINA, a black Kenyan in her late teens/early twenties, suffers a violent attack by a group of British soldiers passing by her village, which leaves her pregnant and HIV-positive. She gives birth to a son, Brad (named after Brad Pitt whom she hopes will adopt the baby with his girlfriend, Angelina Jolie, on their next trip to Africa) and is rejected by her community. Roger, a white Kenyan farmer, found her after the attack and took her to hospital. After her recovery, he employs her as his house servant and soon she is pregnant with his child. At the same time, Roger meets Ronnie, a privileged English girl undertaking research in Africa, who moves in and falls pregnant as well. Ronnie assumes that REGINA's pregnancy is the result of the rape and isn't told that it is Roger's baby. REGINA gives birth to a healthy baby girl, Malaika, but Ronnie's baby is stillborn so she tries to mother Malaika instead. Eventually, REGINA dies from AIDS: throughout the play she returns as a spirit to relive her story. This is the moment when her spirit visits the hospital after Malaika's birth.

REGINA

REGINA as SPIRIT sits on a hospital bed with a copy of 'Hello' magazine. There is a crib next to the bed containing the 'baby'.

Eh heh! Look what I have. It is still here. There is just one magazine in this hospital, it is so dirty and many pages are broken. But this picture it is still here: *(She reads.)* 'Brad Pitt and Angelina Jolie in Africa with their baby, Shiloh.' You know – the first time Bwana Roger brought me to this hospital – to be cleaned from those British – he showed me this picture. He said: 'Look at these people, these are the richest wazungu in the world: they come to Africa to have their babies.' Ayayay! The richest wazungu in the world! Eh heh! They like Africa so much – how can this be? These people wish for their child to be born on African soil because they say 'it is birthplace of all ancestors'. They have travelled to Africa to purchase one orphan girl – and now – you see – they want to come another time in order to purchase one orphan boy to remove to their country. Ayayay! *(Beat.)* And so, you see, I was very happy when my first child was a boy child. Because I knew he would have a very good chance to be selected by these people. *(Beat.)* He did not belong in my village. *(She closes the magazine, gets into bed and peers into the 'cradle'.)*

Also, this name 'Angelina' – tch tch! – I like it very much – it is a mzungu word for 'small angel' which is a very good name, even it can bring many blessings. So I have named my daughter with a Kiswahili word – 'Malaika' – meaning also 'small angel'. This is a good name for her.

MUSWELL HILL
by Torben Betts

This play was first performed at the Orange Tree Theatre, Richmond, on 8 February 2012.

Mat and Jess are having a dinner party at their fashionably decorated home in Muswell Hill. So far, Karen and Simon have arrived. Karen is Jess's slightly-depressed single friend; Simon is an old university friend of Mat's, also single. ANNIE, Jess's younger sister, arrives late. This monologue is her arrival speech: she has just taken some cocaine and so frequently wipes her nose with the back of her hand. Tony arrives soon after, invited by ANNIE. ANNIE (23) and Tony (60) are having an affair: in fact, Annie believes they are engaged (although Tony is already married with adult children). He works in a drama school and seduced Annie with the idea that she could become an actress.

ANNIE

Oh my God I'm so sorry I'm late I had to stay behind at work for an hour and then I set off to get here and I got as far as the tube station but then realised I'd left my bag with my purse and my phone and my Oyster card at the reception desk can you believe and so I had to traipse all the way back to work but when I got there the girl who'd taken over from me had handed the bag into security so I had to go down to the basement where the security office is and I had to speak to this woman there who doesn't like me at all and I had to ask her for my stuff back but she said I had to prove my identity before she'd hand over the bag even though she knows perfectly well who I am cos I've been working there for two months and anyway like I say she made me wait for ages on purpose so she could have her little bit of power over me but then in the end this old guy who is the head of security who I think fancies me a bit he told her off for being such a jobsworth and he let me have my stuff back and so I ran back to the tube and I know I should have called on the way but there was no power left on my phone as it'd been on all day and I hadn't been able to charge it up but anyway listen I'm here now aren't I and oh my God your kitchen I forgot how gorgeous it is it's like something out of a magazine…

…

It really is like something out of *Hello!* and is this a bread-maker I see before me my God I'd die to have a place half as nice as this but anyway I'm talking too much I know I'm a bit nervous so I'll stop now I'm sorry I'm just a bit I just need to simmer down…

MANY MOONS
by Alice Birch

This play was first performed at Theatre503, London, on 17 May 2011.

Many Moons tracks the lives of four lonely people across a day in London. It is JUNIPER's birthday and she wonders if she should invite her neighbour, Oliver, to her party. She dreams of some sort of romantic involvement with him. However, later in the day she discovers him in the local park sexually abusing a small child. This speech occurs at the beginning of the play when we are first introduced to JUNIPER. She speaks directly to the audience.

JUNIPER

I am Looking for Love. I am Actively, looking for Love. You know those traffic light parties where you wear red if you're not available, amber if you might be and green if you absolutely are? Well I'm on green. Constantly.

I sometimes think my Heart will fall Out of my ribcage and land at my feet, the pace at which it beats.

I like a lot of things – I *love* a lot of things. I get excited pretty easily about food and friends and parties and events and the weather and sex and films and just hanging out.

I like Facebook a lot – I have it as an app on my iPhone which I sort of hate, because I like to think of myself as quite an arty kind of person – a bit of a free spirit, even, which is so cheesy but if you knew me you wouldn't think it was so bleugh, you know? I'm a bit cartwheely, a bit sort of out there, you know? I sometimes just get on a train to wherever without buying a ticket and just chat away to whoever I'm next to.

I'd say I was a feminist – but probably not in front of a boyfriend. Not that sexy really, is it? I want to do a bit more, maybe volunteer – there's a shelter not far from me for women and I think I'd be good at that because I am very good at empathising with people. Really. I cry at everything. There was a single mum on *X Factor* with really low self esteem and she had a beautiful voice – a pretty good voice actually – she had a voice – and I just sobbed because I really *felt* for her, you know?

I was going to go on the Reclaim the Night March last year but it was so rainy and there was this Chav Night at this amazing bar in Dalston that I didn't want to miss because there was this boy – but. Anyway. It is an annual thing and I will Definitely go next year, in the diary – I have a five-year diary big pink circle around it.

I have been told I smile a lot. I was once told my smile was my best feature – my bottom is my worst, I know – and I do like to smile. I read somewhere – Glamour, I think – that smiling is statistically proven to be more attractive than makeup…which now I say it out loud sounds ridiculous – I'm not sure how you're supposed to come up with *statistics* for that, but –

Mum worries that I'm not safe – a lot. That I'm too friendly. When I told her I was moving to London she sent me three rape alarms and some mace, which she said was actually surprisingly easy to get hold of once you've figured out how to use Google, when I called her to ask her why she was sending me illegal goods.

I'd never do online dating – you do hear horror stories – and it's so horribly *un*romantic, but I did once put an ad on um Dalston Dating dot com. Just to see.

MOTHERLAND
by Steve Gilroy

This play was first performed at Live Theatre, Newcastle-upon-Tyne on 29 November 2007.

Motherland interweaves verbatim interviews with women who have been affected by the recent conflicts in Iraq and Afghanistan. SUSIE is in her early twenties from Newcastle-upon-Tyne. Her partner, Claire, has joined the army and been sent to war. Here, SUSIE reminisces about their lives together.

SUSIE

Our Mams have always…known each other cos they're both dinner ladies…erm, and they work at the same school so we'd always known each other from when we were quite little. We used to like go round and play.

It was canny really cos I haven't got any brothers or sisters or anything, so I suppose she was…the nearest thing I had to a sister at the time. Erm, but she was a year older than me and I mean…a year's nowt now, but when we were little I thought she was dead cool. She started school before I did, 'n like, she had a boyfriend before I had one and…well not that I ever had a boyfriend like, but y'nah. I just thought that…y'know? I looked up to her like a big sister.

…

And there was one night we'd gotten, gotten a bit, a bit sloshed to be honest…erm…and we just…I don't even remember how it happened actually. To be. Quite, honest I'm, sure she'll kill us for that, don't tell her. Er, I just remember that we were kissing and, everyone was cheering and stuff, you know like they do. *(She cheers.)* I was dead embarrassed, eee I'm embarrassed now talking about it.

Erm, but yeah, so we started kissing and then we just kinda… kissed some more times…and then….and then, we only kissed each other and then we held hands in public and stuff.

…

I think for a while we forgot to tell them: our Mams. But erm, we were just talking about the fact that we were, were moving in and stuff and they were saying: 'Do y'not think that'll be weird living together do y'not think it'll be hard to share a, share a space?' and Claire had said: 'Well other couples share a space.' And there was just this silence.

She was taking her Mam back. 'n my Mam? I went back into the room and she was, just silent. She just didn't say a thing at all. We were just sitting watching the telly and she hadn't said anything about it and all of a sudden she just said: 'Is it my fault?' And I was thinking she was talking about the telly, and I was like: 'Mam what yuh on about man? Is it, is it your fault the telly's on. What?' She was like: 'Is it my fault you're a lesbian. Is it because like, you know, did we do this?'

DEEP CUT
by Philip Ralph

Deep Cut *was commissioned by Sgript Cymru, produced by Sherman Cymru and first performed at Sherman, Cardiff, in 2008.*

Between 1995 and 2002, four young soldiers died from gunshot wounds at their training base, the Deepcut barracks. Their deaths were announced as suicides by the Ministry of Defence, the government and the Surrey police, despite forensic evidence that put this in doubt. The families of these soldiers have been unable to find out what really happened and their calls for a public inquiry have fallen on deaf ears. *Deep Cut* explores the story of eighteen-year-old Cheryl James from Llangollen and her parents' search for the truth about her death. Much of the text is based on first-hand testimonies, including that of another female soldier, JONESY from Rhyl, who joined up around the same time as Cheryl. Here, she talks about how she was recruited.

JONESY

I do believe that everyone who goes in the Army [has] got a reason. Passed my GCSEs and did an A-level. I liked school. But I got in with – well, it wasn't the wrong crowd, we were just a bit loud, I suppose, and we got into fights and we got into a really bad fight one night. We ended up in court and it caused horrendous arguments at home. *(Beat.)* I was just standing there thinking 'My God, I just don't want to end up doing this', you know? 'Cause I knew I wasn't stupid, I'd done my education. And I didn't want to go to university. My mum and stepdad couldn't have afforded [it] anyway. I just didn't know what I wanted to do.

I was 18 [and] I was walking home from school and I was like, 'Bloody hell, I've got no fags, I've got no money, I'm doing a shit job', and there was no jobs in the Job Centre and the ones that were [were] paying like eighty, ninety pounds a week at the time. I did want more. I'll be honest, I wanted more really. And I was walking past the Army careers, I thought, 'My God, I've never noticed that before.' And I went in and the guy in there was eating Kentucky Fried Chicken. He gave me some of his chips [and he] promised me the world and made me watch a video. Oh, God. That was great. So, I signed up there and then. He said I'd have a ball. And to be fair, he didn't lie to me that much, do you know what I mean? [How long did it take] before I signed my life away? Just under twenty minutes, I think.

I had to go and sign my Oath of Allegiance. You have to sign in front of an officer which was really impressive, I thought. And nobody believed I was going to go. Even my friends the night I was due to go in, throwing stones at my bedroom window. They were like, 'You don't want to go in there. It's crap!' but I said, 'I'm going.' That was it. Nothing was stopping me. Stood on the train station, my mum and sisters came [to see me off.] I was crapping myself. *(Beat.)* I arrived at Pirbright on a Sunday afternoon in April.

The main purpose of Pirbright is to make you leave. *(Laughs.)* 'Do you want to go home now?' We'd be like starving and pissed wet through and, you know, wondering why you signed that piece of paper and why did I just get won over by a few scabby Kentucky chips?

BELONGINGS
by Morgan Lloyd Malcolm

*This play was first performed at Hampstead Theatre, London,
on 19 May 2011.*

DEB has returned to her family home in Chippenham after
army service in Afghanistan. Her mother has left and her father
now lives with Jo, whom DEB once had an affair with. She is
forced to confront her feelings about the relationship as well
as what happened to her abroad (one of her male colleagues
brutally raped her). This monologue occurs right at the end
of the play when DEB begins to understand and accept her
mother's actions. She is alone and speaks her thoughts aloud
to the audience.

DEB

When you go out you get your kit and they take your photo. We call them the 'death photos' because they're the ones they will use to send to the press when you're injured or killed. In my last tour they took the photo and I was blinkin'. Fucksake. They were in a rush so they wouldn't let me do another and they were all like 'better make doubly sure you don't get killed then hadn't you?'. It really fucked me off. Because I knew that if I did then I would definitely have my stupid blinkin' photo in every bloody newspaper and then that would be it. That would be the only way people remember me. Because even if there has been multiple deaths you will always get a photo of the female soldier because that's interestin' to folk. That's what sells papers aint it?

Anyway. So yeh. They take your photos. But before that what you do is write your letters. To be opened by your loved ones in the event of your death. Man that was hard. Writin' them. What do you say? With dad's I just basically said a load of mundane shit about lovin' him and 'despite the ups and downs' etcetera. With Jo I told her how I felt and what a wonderful woman I think she is. But with mum. Well for a start it was all a bit bloody academic because we didn't have an address for her so actually I still got the letter with me. But I wanted to still write it. And I said. Well.

She gets the letter out and reads.

Ok. All the usual stuff about missin' her and that. That I love her no matter what. But.

She reads for a moment.

What I didn't write. And what I should have. Was. That I think that she has this, like, massive huge heart inside her and that no one's let her use it properly. And that I'm sorry for not. For not standin' up for her more.

She puts the letter back in her pocket.

I've been covered in this thin film of dust see? Not just in the desert. I've felt like my skin hasn't been able to breathe.

DEB holds her face up to the sun, breathes in and smiles.

PALACE OF THE END
by Judith Thompson

*This play was first performed in London at the Arcola Theatre
on 26 October 2010.*

A twenty-three year old heavily pregnant SOLDIER from West
Virginia tries to defend herself after the world has seen photos
of her torturing Iraqi men in Abu Ghraib prison. The character
is based on the true story of Lynndie England. This monologue
explains the photo of her leading a prisoner around on a dog
leash.

SOLDIER

We was not entertaining ourselves. We was breaking down the terrorists.

And it worked. We did attain information.

…

Takin the guy around on a leash?

Well he called me a dog.

Yes he did. Just like all you losers on the net. He knew a little English and he called me a dog so for once in my life I could fuckin give it to him *you think I'm a dog? You think I'm a fucking dog you monkey fuckin let's go for a fuckin walk you wanna go for a walk?* And Charley and them is laughing and well, I never got laughs before I am not a funny person, and WOW man, getting laughs is the best high the guys was laughing dudes, they loved it, so they go: 'Put him on a leash.' And I do like a sketch, like *Saturday Night Live*, like 'Oh my God it's time to take the dog for a walk… hey Mom? Did you take the dog for a walk? *Henry? Henry.* Did you walk the dog nobody walked the damn dog I'm walkin' it. Here dog, ya dirty dog. No treat for you today you been a *bad dog.*' And I'm pullin him… I was surprised how different is a human neck from a dog neck. With dogs you can pull and pull and they keep on going not with humans. They necks is soft. And… well… It is a weird feeling – made my breathing go – a little funny. Shallow. My voice kinda got full of breath. And I felt like Alice in Wonderland. Where everything was not real and I could walk out again anytime and what was behind there would stay there.

AFTER THE END
by Dennis Kelly

This play was first performed at the Bush Theatre in a Paines Plough/Bush Theatre co-production on 28 July 2005.

Mark and LOUISE were trapped in a fallout shelter in Mark's backyard for a number of days. Mark told LOUISE that he rescued her after a nuclear attack but in reality he had kidnapped her. Not only did he limit her food rations but raped and tried to kill her. After she was rescued, LOUISE visits Mark in prison. Her ordeal has disoriented her and she feels disconnected from friends, family and work colleagues. Despite her hatred of Mark, he is the only one she can really talk to now.

LOUISE

I think a lot about what makes people do things. What makes
us behave in certain ways, you know. Every night I been
thinking about this. Trapped in whatever, behaviour, I dunno,
cycles of violence or something and is it possible to break,
these cycles, is it possible to break… And I'd be sitting there
thinking about this and this cat, this gorgeous cat with no tail
would come to my door. I'd have the back door open because
the garden looks, and she'd be terrified at first, it looks
beautiful it really does. So I bought some food for her and
the first time she just sniffed at it and ran away, the moment
I moved, you know, no sign of her for the rest of the night,
and I'm thinking, reactions and responses, patterns, violence
breeding violence, and the next night she's in a bit further
and I'm looking at her tail thinking 'that's been cut off' and
I don't think it was, I think she's a Manx, I think they're
born without tails, and the next night she's further in and
I'm beginning to get used to this, beginning to look forward
to it. And the next night she's in and she's eating and from
then on she's in every night; she's on my lap, she's following
me around, she's waiting on the window ledge for me when
I get home. And we sit there every night and I'm thinking
behaviour and patterns and is it actually possible to break
these patterns or whatever and she's eating and meowing to
be let in. Every night. And one night she scratches me, out of
the blue, cats, you know, just a vindictive cat-scratch, look:

Shows him.

see?

…

She knew she'd done wrong.

Took her three nights to get back into my lap. And I'm stroking her and thinking. Warm, delicate, you know. And I put my hands around her neck. And I squeeze. And I squeeze. Until her neck is about the thickness of a rope. And still I squeeze. And I'm sitting there – and this is last night – with this dead cat in my lap, and I thought I'd come in and see you.

And here I am.

DEEP HEAT
by Robin Soans

Selections from Deep Heat *were first performed at a National Theatre Platform in London on 9 May 2011.*

Deep Heat, subtitled 'Encounters with the Famous, the Infamous and the Unknown', contains verbatim monologues collected and edited by Robin Soans. The following excerpt is the written voice of twenty-five year old CAROLINE KENDAL, who hosts a radio programme featuring world music. Here we find her in the middle of one of her shows, sitting in a studio with headphones on. She introduces a musical track then removes her headphones to talk to the interviewer about her road rage experiences.

CAROLINE

I'm Caroline Kendall with two hours of world music and it's just coming up to nine minutes to five o'clock; and to take us up to the news, weather and the latest sports news and to put you in a romantic mood for the evening ahead, we have three Brazilian love songs with the generic title *Come se voce estivesse la* sung by Las Columbinas, and the girls' voices are accompanied by nose-flutes, pan pipes, guitar, djembes, and the soft serenading of viola de gamba; so light a candle, open the red wine, and allow yourself to melt into the full embrace of Latin magic… *(Headphones off.)*

My road rage continues onwards and upwards. My anger knows no bounds. I'll tangle with anything…giant buses, inter-continental juggernauts ferrying carcasses of frozen beef… it's a disorder…I have to get them back…even if someone's just looked at me. I was in Greenwich. I had the window down…these two scuzz-bags drew alongside…gave me that look…'Get your tits out'…I gave them a filthy look, so they pushed in front. We went racing round…at the next lights I shouted, 'Where did you get your driving license…the same place you got your shirts?' They were wearing these crimplene shirts…one in orange, the other in pink, and they looked like Teletubbies only slightly less attractive…and the orange Teletubby got out and kicked the front of my car, and got back in again, and started driving off…my car's called Pascal, named after a Swiss chef, and I thought, 'Those bastards have dented Pascal' and I chased them. My car horn wore out. George at the garage said he'd never known a horn wear out before. There we were at eighty miles an hour narrowly

missing old ladies and packs of Brownies…I was shouting at
them…'Bastard fucking Teletubby miscreant shit-bags'…got
their number…we did two double-U turns on Tower Bridge…
ended up outside Sadler's Wells. They stopped their car, so I
stopped mine…felt a bit stupid now, cos I didn't know what
I was going to do really. This time the pink Teletubby got
out, came over to my car, ripped the car keys out and threw
them in a hedge, and then pulled me out through the driver's
window, and dumped me on the pavement, and then drove
off. I had bruises all up my thighs…I had to be at work in
forty minutes to do my evening show…frantically phoning the
police. A week later PC Plod came round to do the business,
and then a week later I got a letter saying, 'We're not going
to pursue this.' I phoned back saying, 'What the fuck are
you playing at? Innocent female etc. etc.' and demanded to
be put on to someone more senior…and then more senior…
eventually got to the bloke with five hundred pips on his
shoulder, and he said, 'The thing is, those two men were part
of the Brinks Matt Robbery Gang, and they're going down
for twenty-five years anyway. It's not really worth trying to
get another six months on the sentence for menacing you.'
It turns out the man who pulled me through the window
was the third most dangerous man in Europe. I didn't chase
anyone for a week after that.

BLUE HEART AFTERNOON
by Nigel Gearing

Blue Heart Afternoon *was first performed at Hampstead Theatre, London, on 5 April 2012.*

It's Hollywood, 1951 and the INGENUE (aka Jennifer) is an aspiring actress in her twenties from Texas who is sleeping with a successful songwriter (Ernie Case). He believes that she is trying to bargain her way into his next project with the Studio. However, it seems that she is working undercover for Senator McCarthy's anti-communist witch hunt and he isn't the only one she has been 'spying on'. In this monologue, in which she speaks directly to the audience, we learn a little more about her life before Hollywood.

INGENUE

So there we were, Mom and me – see, Mom was my 'chaperone', and we all had to have a 'chaperone' – there we were the two of us, bussed over to Austin real nice and put up in this swell hotel. 'Cept the Event itself, this was in an indoor stadium, and when we first got there they told us how it worked, what we had to do – they called this The Induction – so soon I learned there was as many as thirty of us all told but Mom said, 'No question! Talent? Personality? Poise? Did God really <u>want</u> me to be second-bested by Lois Greenberg?'

Well, that first day we had to rehearse like crazy until they held the Swimsuit part of the competition, and you walk out on your high heels along this ramp to a circle, praying you won't fall over, remembering like you got an imaginary string holding your head erect, remembering you got to <u>glide</u> and neither swing the arms too much or hold them too stiff neither 'cos that'd make things just as worse, and always afraid the swimsuit it's riding up at the back where you forgot to tape it but you don't dare reach back and pull it down with all them hundreds of eyes on you, not to mention the photographers, and you turn once ever so slowly so the judges <u>and</u> the crowd <u>and </u>the photographers they can get a good look at your ankles and your thighs and your ass. (Of course, Lois Greenberg said this was all 'degrading'. Naturally she would! I ask you: what's 'degrading' about your ass unless it looks like Lois Greenberg's?)

And so then after another day's rehearsal came the last and major Event – full evening-gown and four-button-gloves 'n' all – and all the flashing bulbs and all the people out there, this time in their tuxedos, and there was this big banquet before the main show – can you believe it? I mean, I couldn't eat a thing if they was paying me, which I guess in a way they was! – and then an introduction by the Mayor and – hey! that's when I first heard Mr Case's song? 'Blue Heart Afternoon?' – full orchestra and all! They said it was the Song Of the Year!... Before I knew it, we were down to ten and then five, would you believe, and – some reason I don't understand, Lois Greenberg, she was still in there, hair down to her shoulders like some dime-store Veronica Lake and so padded out front it made you feel you was about to be run over – and then each of us was asked to speak for one minute no more no less to the gentleman holding a microphone, they called him 'The Master Of Ceremonies, on 'How Would You Make The World A Better Place?'

Lois Greenberg was ahead of me and, of course, she said with that stuck-up goodie-goodie voice of hers she's had since Junior High, 'I think we should just learn to love each other a little more, all creeds, religions and races…' I mean – Yuh! Pass me the sick bag, right? So when it came to my turn 'Tell us, Jennifer: How Would You Make The World A Better Place?' I was about to say, 'Well, you could start by pushing Lois Greenberg off a cliff,' but, see, I was smart, I told them good and straight: 'I don't know too much about them other creeds, religions and races. All I know as a true American is that now more than ever we gotta defend ourselves against them out there who want to destroy this the best Country in the World, with this the best Way of Life in the World…'

…And, well, tra-la-la, that's how I came to win 'Miss Texas 1950'. 'Cos win it I truly did. And, well, – there you have the whole story of me thinking, Jennifer my girl, from here on out it's only a short step to Movie-Stardom, and then me coming out here to Hollywood and…as for Lois Greenberg – <u>Who</u>??

LULLABIES OF BROADMOOR:
THE MURDER CLUB
by Steve Hennessy

The Murder Club *is one of four plays published under the title
of* Lullabies of Broadmoor *and was first produced by Theatre
West in November 2003.*

All four plays in 'Lullabies of Broadmoor' are based on true
stories of Broadmoor inmates during the late nineteenth and
early twentieth centuries. *The Murder Club* focuses on Richard
Prince, who murdered the theatre matinee idol, William
Terriss, in 1897 (and was a Broadmoor patient between 1897
and 1937), and Ronald True who murdered the prostitute
OLIVE YOUNG in 1922 (and was a Broadmoor patient from
1922 until 1951). OLIVE was christened Gertrude Yates but
changed her name after becoming a prostitute. She was 25
years old when Ronald True smashed her skull in. She opens
the play as a ghost with the following monologue.

OLIVE

(Whispers.) Mother!

That's the most common last word of soldiers on the battlefield apparently. Natural I suppose, surrounded by fear and blood and death. But why was it my last word? I hated the stuck-up cow! We had our final falling out when I decided on a career change which would half my hours and double my wages. Oh, mother didn't mind me working twelve hours a day at the fur store, being goosed up by the manager every five minutes! But she wasn't happy with my new job where men paid for the privilege. 'You've destroyed my happiness, Gertrude! If your father finds out, it will kill him! If the neighbours find out, we'll have to move! At least do the right thing now! Don't ever show your face in this house again. Go now, and go quietly.'

Yes, mother loved melodrama! And murder mysteries. Her favourite actor was William Terriss. She'd see his shows over and over again. Had the hots for him I imagine. She loved romance! No, darlings, it don't run in the family. But the year I was born, Terriss was stabbed to death. 'I cried for days. The funeral route was lined with women crying. You could barely get into the cemetery! Proper man, he was my dear. Handsome, kind. Gave money to all the out of work actors, even the actor who killed him and do you know what Richard Prince did with that money? Went straight out and bought a knife to murder him with. I can't bear to watch murder mysteries any more!' Mother queued for hours to get into the trial so she could get a look at the murderer. They all hissed like it was the panto villain when he came into court. He loved that, apparently. Twenty years after Terriss died, mother was still going on about him! 'To think I actually saw him stabbed on stage! Poor Mercutio! Such beautiful death scenes, Romeo and Juliet!' I got so sick of listening to her guff, one day I said, 'Bet the real thing weren't so pretty? That loony with the knife up a dirty alleyway?' She never mentioned his name again. I always thought there was too much prettifying of murder, even before I was done in. And if I'm ever going to understand why it happened, it's more important than ever to see things as they really are.

Which is why I'm here! In Broadmoor Criminal Lunatic Asylum, with Richard Prince, and Mr. Coleman, principal attendant, Gentlemen's Block. Ronald True, the man who caved in my skull with a rolling pin will be along in a minute. Funny how things work out, isn't it?

BODIES UNFINISHED
by Lewis Hetherington

*This play was first performed by Grey Swan at the Brockley
Jack Studio Theatre on 14 July 2011.*

STELLA is an escort in her twenties. Alan, whose life is in a
mess, thinks he is in love with STELLA after a series of 'dates'
and asks her to move in with him. However, it all goes horribly
wrong. Alan hates the thought of her having been with so many
men and he can't get it out of his head. In this monologue, we
hear how STELLA really feels about her past.

STELLA

I've had so many men in me it's like my insides have been fucked out.

I've had men who fuck me until I'm empty, who fuck me like they're fighting a war, fuck me to split me up the middle, fuck me until I'm useless, a boneless wreck shattered across the bed.

And yes I play along every time
I lie on the bed like he has overpowered me
play dead for him as he zips up his trousers
breathe urgently as he empties his wallet on the bedside table
wrap my arms around my body as though I'm holding myself together.

I can never bare to look at them afterwards
So I cower a little
let you believe I'm terrified to look into your eyes
as though one look and I'd collapse into a puddle on the floor.

I pull my clothes on and feel your taste in my mouth
I want to spit you, your taste, out of my mouth.

And then you
Tug at your shirt sleeves adjust your tie
I smile.
And when the door clicks shut I hold still for as long as I can.
Try and scratch your face out of my brain
hold my breath to fill me up
but there's always something left.

I have to live with all those men still inside me. Not you.

WE'RE GONNA MAKE YOU WHOLE
by Yasmine Van Wilt

We're Gonna Make You Whole *was first performed at the Acquire Arts in Battersea, London on 10 August 2011.*

This play is based on the true-life testimonies of Louisiana residents who were affected by a major petrochemical disaster. KELLY is in her mid- to late twenties and was working in the fishing industry with her husband before the oil rig exploded. Now business is at a standstill because of the environmental consequences of the disaster: their recent catches have been affected by oil pollution and are inedible. In this monologue she describes, as part of her testimony, exactly what she has seen and experienced.

KELLY

I don't really know what you need for the testimony. Do you – do you plan to make the records public? Okay. Well. Ha… They say: 'We're gonna make you whole.' That is straight-up bullshit. *(Beat.)* What have they offered? *(Beat.)* Well…about thirty. *(Beat.)* We made a hundred grand last year. We paid off the house. *(Beat.)* Of course we can't crab anymore. *(Beat.)* NO – If I won't eat the crabs or the oysters, how am I gonna feel good about myself if I'm selling them to other people, knowing what's in 'em. The crabs we pick up, they're black on the inside. You crack the shells…and you can smell the oil. I wouldn't want my nieces and nephews eating it. *(Beat.)* Hard to believe people think all that oil just disappeared. *(Beat.)* Shrimp – they're like the cockroaches of the sea. They're delicious, but they are – bottom feeders. *(Beat.)* And they just sponge in all those oils and toxins – all that crap from the dispersants *(Beat.)* You get the shrimp, out of the water, you can see them lined, all the insides, they look like they smoked thirty years. What people don't know is that THE Company are running a secret, giant, free abortion clinic. Right now, I'd actually like to have those freaks – you know the ones that campaign at the offices – that throw paint at the doctors – I'd like to have them on my side. *(Beat.)* I…was three months. When I…lost the baby. I was…still…I was nervous about… being a mother. I wasn't sure I'd know what to do. I'm almost glad it's dead. Because what kind of a world is this. I've had friends…who also… And my sister. Her – she just had a little girl Shelly. And she has birth defects. They don't know if… *(Beat.)* She's so small, you can only touch her with one finger through the incubator... She's – I almost don't know what's worse. You get more attached when they're...they're older and they... It's not a question a mother ever wants to rationalise...

I recently tried to get the attention of THE Company. And... all anyone can ask me is, 'did I feel like I was supported.' 'Do I think it made a difference?'

Well, what do you think? I wouldn't have had to...walk 1200 miles to get them to listen if they were open to suggestion. *(Beat.)* I don't think this is one person's fault. This...is a whole system broke down.

(Beat.) I get in my boat, down Barrataria Bay, and I don't hear – egrets calling. I don't see the tails of fish twitching on the horizon. I don't...there isn't much of anything. Except the stink of oil, and – the burn, of your eyes going dull because Corexit is eating your flesh. Most people...they don't understand...

THE DREYFUS AFFAIR: A TRILOGY
by George R. Whyte

Dreyfus Intime *was first performed at the Opernhaus Zurich on 22 December 2007.* Rage and Outrage *was first performed on ARTE/Channel 4 in April 1994.* The Dreyfus Affair *was first performed at Deutsche Oper Berlin on 8 May 1994.*

This trilogy of plays explores the true story of Alfred Dreyfus, who was a Jewish officer in the French army in the late nineteenth century. He was stripped of his title and incarcerated for many years on Devil's Island on the trumped up charge of espionage, sparking a frenzy of anti-Jewish feeling across France. This monologue has been taken from the first play in the trilogy, *Dreyfus Intime*, which uses letters and diary entries to reveal events and characters. In the following letter, LUCIE asks her husband to approach his future with strength and bravery. Soon afterwards Dreyfus was found guilty in a public ceremony by the Ecole Militaire in Paris, evoking violent anti-Semitism in the watching crowds.

LUCIE

My dear husband.

You know that I love you, that I adore you, my own dear husband; our intense grief, the horrible infamy of which we are the object, do nothing but tighten the links of my affection.

Wherever you go, wherever they send you, I will follow you;

We shall bear exile more easily together, we will live for each other…; we will educate our children, we will give them a soul well fortified against the vicissitudes of life.

I cannot do without you, you are my consolation; the only gleam of happiness that is left me is to finish my days by your side. You have been a martyr, and you have still to suffer horribly. The punishment which will be inflicted on you is odious. Promise me that you will bear it bravely.

You are strong in your innocence; accept the unmerited punishment; do it for me, for the wife who loves you. Give her this proof of affection, do it for your children; they will be grateful to you one day. The poor children embrace you, and often ask for their papa.

Once more, courage! You must live for our children, for me.

I suffer beyond anything that you can imagine on account of the horrible tortures that you are undergoing; my thoughts do not leave you for a moment. I see you alone in your sad prison, a prey to the most gloomy reflections; I compare our years of happiness, the sweet days we spent together, with the present time. How happy we were, how good and devoted you were to me! With what perfect devotion you cared for me when I was ill, what a father you have been to our poor darlings! All this passes and repasses in my mind; I am unhappy at not having you with me, at being alone. My dear loved one, we must, we absolutely must, be together again; we must live for each other, for we cannot exist without each other.

I weep and weep, and then weep again. Your letters alone bring me consolation in my great grief; they alone sustain me and comfort me. Live for me, I entreat you, my dear friend; gather up your strength, and strive – we will strive together until the guilty man is found.

I am asking an enormous sacrifice of you, that of living for me, for our children, of striving for reinstatement… I should die of grief if you were no more, I should not have the strength to continue a struggle for which you alone of all the world can strengthen me.

Go through the sad ceremony bravely, raise your head and proclaim your innocence, your martyrdom, in the faces of your executioners.

PART THREE: THIRTIES

JOY AND TYRANNY
by Arnold Wesker

At the time of going to press, Joy and Tyranny *had not received a professional production.*

Wesker describes *Joy and Tyranny* as 'arias and variations on the theme of violence', where different characters explore their thoughts on power, force, aggression, hostility, brutality and cruelty. The COMEDIENNE is thirty years old and is talking to an outdoor audience at Speakers' Corner in Hyde Park in London.

COMEDIENNE

Here's my problem – I'm a singer on the verge of giving
up singing to try my hand at stand-up comedy, but no one
thinks I'm very funny so I may have to stick with singing.
I'm not a bad singer, in fact in certain quarters I've got a cult
following. No, I'm not going to sing to you, you'll just have to
take my word for it, but here's my dilemma: I'm also a single
mother and I have this daughter, Juniper, who I feel guilty for
neglecting when I go on gigs, so I'm writing a letter for her to
read when she's fourteen. It started as a letter of apology for
being a bad mum but it's turning into a letter of advice. So far
I've advised her on four counts.

The fourth, and perhaps the most important piece of advice,
is about choosing her peers, and here's where I'd like *your*
advice about *my* advice to my daughter. 'Select your peers,'
I want to tell her. 'Don't go with the herd. Don't look to be

one of the gang. I know there's great comfort in a gang,' I
want to tell her, 'in belonging, in being accepted but – resist
it! A gang,' I want to warn her, 'is made up of people who are
living their lives through each other'. I know! I was part of a
gang, one of the girls, always busy being what I thought would
please the others, picking up their bad habits, thinking their
thoughts, sharing their stupid prejudices, laughing with them
at their mindless hatreds. We never questioned each other,
we just raised our arms and clenched our fists and stroked
each other's nonsense, terrified of stepping out of line. Not
one of us had an opinion that was our own. Not one of us
was independent. And we intimidated each other. If one of
us dared to say 'I don't agree! I don't think we should,' out
would come that dreary old cry: *'Who do you think you are?'*

I think I hate that cry more than any other in the whole wide
world, ladies and gentlemen. So I want to warn her: If anyone
cries it out to you, Juniper, you tell them: Juniper thinks she's
an individual! She thinks she can think her own thoughts!
She thinks she can rise above the herd! You tell them that,
sweetheart.

And then I change my mind. No! Don't, I should be telling
her. They'll slaughter you! Whatever you do, don't stand
above the herd. In fact don't even think of them as a herd.
They are *not* a herd, a herd is a collection of dumb animals.
They're not dumb animals. They're your *(Sardonically.)*
brothers and sisters, your comrades in arms, your link to
reality, your support system. I should be advising her to stay
with them, stay with them or they'll tear you limb from limb.

Then I change my mind again. 'Take the risk!' I want to yell. 'Stand out! Fly... Fly I want to advise her, don't join the herd. Am I right? Should I be urging my only daughter to take risks and fly, to stand out above the herd, the crowd, the mob, go against the drift of things? Is the world divided between the mob and the risk-takers? Is it? Tell me. I'm asking you.

MARY MASSACRE
by *Johnny McKnight*

Mary Massacre *is part of* Double Nugget, *first performed by Random Accomplice at the Tron Theatre, Glasgow on 14 February 2012.*

Mary Massacre intertwines the stories of LEYLA and Jenny: two disappointed women from Glasgow. LEYLA describes herself as '30…ish'. All her friends are married and she feels her biological clock ticking over: internet dating seems like the answer. In this monologue, LEYLA describes (for the audience) one of her less-than-successful attempts to meet up with a man she has met online.

LEYLA

Online dating is slightly weird. You've only got their picture to go on, of course that's assuming it is an actual picture of themselves. That and the profile description. I mean it's not like you can hear them. They could look like David Beckham but they might have a voice to match.

…

What first attracted me to Mark was his punctuation. He knew his commas, knew the difference between the three theres. He even spelt accommodation correctly.

I felt it was cyber-destiny.

He was 35, worked in Managerial Consultancy and lived in Troon.

Now there are rules to meeting strangers.

If you're in any way unsure I'd suggest a bit of research at www.kissmegoodnight.com forward slash 30 plus and gagging for a man.

Meet somewhere public and well-lit. I opted for the art gallery in Glasgow – the website felt that 'visual stimulus was a real opportunity for love to blossom.' I also did a bit of research re. what paintings would be there so I could show off a wee bit and look knowledgeable. 'Oh Mark! A Beryl Cook – do you know she died? Terrible loss. Victoria Wood's a fan, you know! Calls them Rubens with jokes.' Makes me look cultured.

Mark told me he would be wearing a black suit with red tie. I thought it a good sign that he knew what he'd be wearing in advance, shows decisiveness, and I like that in a man.

I, obviously, didn't have a clue on my outfit so I told him to look out for a leggy brunette with a dazzling personality. I thought he might have laughed at that, instead he asked if I would be wearing a jacket. Depends on the weather I said.

…

A disaster is probably the best way to describe him, it. As soon as I saw Mark I thought – this just won't do. This just isn't me. It was his eyes – the way he looked at you made you feel uneasy. Like he was looking just a bit too closely. Janice said that was because he was boss-eyed. Oh that's the other thing about a blind date – always have a friend on standby. Someone waiting at another end of the art gallery to ring your mobile with a fake emergency.

No point wasting time. Babies to be made, houses to be bought.

MARY MASSACRE
by *Johnny McKnight*

Mary Massacre is part of Double Nugget*, first performed by Random Accomplice at the Tron Theatre, Glasgow on 14 February 2012.*

Mary Massacre intertwines the stories of Leyla and JENNY: two women from Glasgow with disappointing lives. JENNY is unhappily married to Gavin who has been chatting with Leyla on an internet dating service. Leyla and Gavin agree to meet at Marymass Fair, where JENNY is filling in as a fortune teller. Leyla has a few minutes to spare before the rendezvous and decides to have her fortune read. When Gavin appears at the tent, JENNY conjures up the word 'Grace' on the Ouija board. The following is her inner monologue, remembering what happened to their child.

JENNY

Grace.

Say the name and that feeling's back. And the face.

Her face.

The face that tells you you'll never be good enough for him.

Who'd want a wife like you? A mother like you?

Who'd leave their kid to play alone outside?

A scream.

Thud.

The thud of falling.

Hushed quiet.

Then…

Quiet. But really quiet, the quiet that only a mother fears.

I knew as soon as I saw her.

I knew.

It was her face.

Her wee face.

As soon as I picked her up.

I knew.

She looked.

I remember.

Shocked.

It was as though she had done something wrong.

The gate just swinging open.

She looked guilty.

I kept saying it's okay.

Okay.

We'll be okay.

That fucking woman just standing over her car.

Screaming.

No, not screaming.

Howling.

Like a dog.

Grace.

Whimpering.

That wee face.

Burst.

I still phoned.

999.

But I knew.

I could feel her in my arms.

It was like her.

She just kept.

Getting lighter.

Her hands were just.

It was like she was trying to grab hold of something.

And I was squeezing those wee hands.

Trying to give her something to hold on to.

But I just never.

Never squeezed hard enough.

For her.

Phillip and Fern laughing away in the background.

Gavin singing in the shower upstairs.

Her outside howling.

Me.

I don't know what I was.

Mad.

Crying.

And she just disappeared.

I don't even remember when she went.

I couldn't see her face for crying.

Never got to see her.

Go.

Vanish.

Grace.

ORPHANS
by Dennis Kelly

*This play was first performed at the Traverse Theatre,
Edinburgh on 31 July 2009.*

Siblings, HELEN and Liam, were orphaned at an early age and
brought up in care. HELEN has her own family now: husband,
Danny, and, son, Shane. She is also pregnant again. The play
opens when Liam turns up on HELEN's and Danny's doorstep
covered in blood, claiming to have found a young lad injured
on the street. Her first instinct is to protect him. However,
Liam's story changes each time HELEN and Danny probe for
details. Eventually it emerges that Liam has assaulted an Asian
man who is tied up in a friend's shed. Helen talks Danny into
helping by scaring the man into silence. On Danny's return,
HELEN sees that she has forced him down to Liam's level
of violence. In this excerpt, she is angry and tells Liam that,
far from being the ever-loyal sister, she once tried to separate
herself from him. Liam had always thought this was a lie told
by one of their school friends, Brian, and had beaten him for it.
Now he learns it is the truth. Finally, HELEN throws Liam out,
hoping to start life afresh; however, it appears her relationship
with Danny has been irrevocably damaged.

HELEN

I was going to go with that family.

> *Beat.*

Brian was right. I told him, because I was so excited. I had to tell someone.

> *Beat.*

…

His name was John, hers was Jackie, John and Jackie, they lived in a lovely place, I remember, green and I remember the road was…lovely.

…

They had a boy a little older than me, Adam, he had a tree house in the garden, but it wasn't in a tree it was on the ground, they'd built it for him on the ground because he didn't like heights but it was all his, they never went in there, they respected his space.

> *Beat.*

…

She had a job, I don't remember what it was, but I remember she had it because mum never had a job, she just sat around smoking, he was a doctor and I thought that was amazing, that someone's dad could really be a doctor. And his face was lovely. He had a lovely face, I don't remember his face but it was lovely and their house was clean, not like our house, our house was filthy, I played a game with them, a board-game, I don't remember what it was, but we all sat down and played it together and I was amazed, all of us, just sitting there playing this game, John and Jackie as well.

Beat.

Adam kept showing me things. And telling me things. Things I didn't know, I didn't know them and he could tell I didn't know them but he never laughed at me, never once, he never once laughed at me for not knowing. He just told me things, all these things, and he showed me his rabbit. He let me hold her. She was soft and warm and I held her for ages, for ages, I just held her for ages, and I started crying, I was holding his rabbit and crying and he didn't say anything, he just let me, he just let me hold her and cry for ages and ages and ages and ages.

…

I loved them.

…

I begged them to let me go with them. But after you attacked Brian we got moved away. I begged and begged and begged.

MIXED UP NORTH
by Robin Soans

The first professional production of Mixed Up North *was at the Octagon Theatre in Bolton on 10 September 2009.*

Mixed Up North documents the journey of a youth theatre group in Burnley, Lancashire, set up to help bridge the gap between Asian and white teenagers. ANEESA is a 32-year-old trainee youth worker involved with the project. She is in an arranged marriage with an 11-month-old son. Her parents found a husband for her in Pakistan after realising she was seeing somebody who was six years older and separated from his wife and child. However, ANEESA did receive a university education prior to her marriage. In this monologue she explains to some of the other youth workers how this came about.

ANEESA

At one stage I never thought I'd end up with a worthwhile job. My eldest sister…this is literally how her life went… school, 'til she was sixteen, job from 16 to 19, packing up bottles of bleach on a conveyor belt, then off to Pakistan into an arranged marriage to her first cousin, came back, went through the palaver of getting him British Citizenship and had her first child within ten months of being married.

…

And yes, that is how it was going to be for me…school, bleach, marriage…no chance of further education…that's your life…bang…no questions asked.

…

We weren't encouraged to do our homework.

…

You're going into an arranged marriage as soon as possible… your life will be bringing up children and looking after your own parents and your husband's parents…what do you need education for?

…

My second oldest sister was the one who fought for an education…massive hoo-hah at home…shouting, screaming, swearing…you'd think she'd come home and said she'd got pregnant…my brothers joining in…it was mi brothers that scared us more than mi mum and dad…not just elder brothers, but younger brothers as well. They saw it as their duty to uphold the family honour, and that meant no stepping out of line. That's the biggest thing which lets our community down... 'What would people think if you step one hairsbreadth out of line?' Mi mum's line was, 'Where did I go wrong? Why does this always happen to me?' Mi father said mi sister was betraying the whole family.

...

By sheer doggedness, mi sister won in the end. She went to Leeds University to study psychology. My next sister, instead of saying, 'I want to go to University' she said, 'I am going to University.' By the time it got to me, my parents said, 'You will go to University, and you will read psychology'...mi father all proud going round telling people, 'Oh mi daughter's gone to University. We're a very progressive family.' Though mi elder sister who started it off...she's a University lecturer now...she's got a great career...but because she's thirty-seven and not married, people say she must be either mad, a witch or a pervert.

MY BEST FRIEND
by Tamsin Oglesby

This play was first performed at Hampstead Theatre in London on 20 January 2000.

Best friends, Bee and Em, are holidaying in rural France. However, their time together is shattered by CHRIS who turns up unexpectedly (or so Bee thinks). All three women are now in their thirties and school memories are hazy and ill-remembered, leading to a fractious evening with a number of vicious revelations. In this scene, CHRIS arrives at the house with a story to tell about her journey. Typically, she isn't able to stop talking, filling the uncomfortable shock of her presence with a stream of (oblivious) words.

CHRIS

Oh thank god it's you darling/

…

Thought I'd got the wrong house, taxi's gone disaster. Although frankly, quite frankly, I'd rather play murder in the dark with a machete than get back in the car with that horrid little Frenchman. I've just had the most ghastly journey with this man. You know what I'm like, always choose the duffers – trust me – I sail straight past a queue of gorgeous pouting frogs and get into the cab of a toad. God I'm exhausted. All the way from Avignon he leered at me and then he seemed to think – when he asked me what I did and I said 'research' – he seemed to think I'd be up for a shag in the back of his car! God knows what I said, obviously means complete fucking tart in French. So he stopped in the middle of nowhere – for a slash, he said, 'pour faire aggrandir l'herbe', you know, and he disappeared for bloody ages, obviously expecting me to follow him, if you please, so I sat there thinking, 'nobody knows I'm here, oh my god, I'm going to die and become a statistic' and then eventually he emerges from the shrub ostentatiously wiping his hands, like this, wiping the spunk off his hands, you know, *disgusting*, dirty great smirk on his face, and then he gets in the car and he doesn't stop talking.

…

All the way here, gabbing like radio Luxembourg and every time he stops at a light he puts his hand on my knee – made me sit in the front, I don't know, maybe that's what taxi drivers do in France, I thought, bloody pervert, let me out of here. I feel completely and utterly invaded I can tell you.

…

…happens to me all the time. *(She strides about the verandah.)* Well this is alright, isn't it? I like the red. Very distressed-chic. It's a sort of barn, isn't it really?

MY BEST FRIEND
by Tamsin Oglesby

This play was first performed at Hampstead Theatre in London on 20 January 2000.

Best friends EM and Bee are holidaying in rural France. However, their time together is shattered by Chris who turns up unexpectedly (or so Bee thinks). All three women are now in their thirties and school memories are hazy and ill-remembered, leading to a fractious evening with a number of vicious revelations. EM is the only one of them that has a husband and children but finds her life difficult. In this monologue, she tries to explain.

EM

You think it's original, don't you, at that age, you think you're the only ones, that you're so clever, but Louis – eleven years old he is and he's started, he's already started with this made-up language, he does it with this particular friend, they start gibbering and he loves the fact that I don't know what they're on about, he just loves it, the little bugger. They come in, him and his friend, and this boy, Ed, keeps going 'I nac ees roy srekin' every time I see him, it's so annoying, I mean I could easily, if I wanted, I could easily work out what they're saying, but I can't be bothered, wittering away about trainers or gameboy or whatever it is, because they have this life, you see, this other life suddenly, and you're expected to – I don't know what. Skivvy. Shuttup and do the dishes. And then you're wheeled in for a bit of maths homework (which, in my case is a joke, of course) but you're *no fun* any more. What you are, what you become to them, it has nothing to do with fun. I'm not complaining. Because of course in Tom's case I'm still a walking breast and Martha's only just out of nappies so there's all that, but sometimes – I mean, even Martha, I said to her the other week, she wouldn't wear this lovely yellow dress because her friend Morgan apparently doesn't like yellow and I said 'it doesn't matter what other people think. It's what you think that matters'. A few days later she wouldn't put on this hat and we had this argument; 'Why not?' 'Don't like it.' 'Well I love it' I said. 'I don't care what you think. It's what I think that matters'. I felt about as big as the gap under the door. I mean, God, I love them to death, but sometimes it just feels like need, rejection, need, rejection, nothing in between you know, nothing adult – well, Cob obviously – but when you're shovelling cold baked beans in your mouth straight from the tin because you just haven't got time, and your clothes are covered in crap and back to front, you think, hang on, hang on a minute, what about me? What about me? I'm not complaining, it's just, it's just… *(She stops suddenly in mid-thought.)* back to front, of course, it's back to front! 'I nac ees roy srekin'. 'I can…see…your…knickers', oh god, 'I can see your knickers' back to front, 'I nac ees roy srekin.'

EM begins to laugh. The laugh gets louder and longer and longer until it's out of control. And then, to the amazement of BEE and CHRIS, it turns into a wail, and EM cries uncontrollably.

THE PROPHET
by Hassan Abdulrazzak

The Prophet *received its UK premiere at the Gate Theatre,
Notting Hill on 14 June 2012.*

In 2011, Egypt erupted into revolution. LAYLA and Hisham,
a middle class couple in their 30s, live in downtown Cairo. On
28th January, Hisham (a writer) chooses to attend a meeting
with an important potential agent rather than join the protest.
However, LAYLA (head engineer at a telecommunications
company) decides to go, ignoring her boss who wants the
mobile phone network shut down (after a visit from state
security). In this monologue we find LAYLA on the streets and
surprised by how the poor have joined the middle classes in a
united revolution.

LAYLA

…when I got off at Mubarak I was immediately suffocated with tear gas. The police had fired tear gas into the metro station, never mind it was named after our beloved president, that didn't stop them. Everybody was now running out. I went past police with their guard dogs. I couldn't breathe. My eyes were hurting. All exits were shut except one. The police were dictating the direction we were going. When I emerged from the exit, I had no idea where I was. Then it dawned on me that I was in the type of neighbourhood we call ashwaiya, meaning that it is a slum inhabited by the very poor of Cairo.

Pause.

So picture the scene, a group of suffocated, mainly middle-class Cairenes like myself emerging out of the metro station in the heart of the Egyptian underclass. Marx must have been dancing in his grave with joy. Before me I saw a massive crowd, all determined to head to Tahrir Square but the streets leading out of the ashwaiya slum were blocked by police. How to get there? And that's when I saw her, a girl of sixteen or seventeen, a street girl with a gash on her cheek, the type that sells Kleenex tissue at traffic lights. She was guiding us disorientated demonstrators towards Tahrir. She would run ahead of us, check out the street to see if it is blocked by the police then run back and lead us through yet another alleyway. We kept snaking our way through the slum until we emerged on a main road. Ahead of us was the Hilton hotel which seemed like a mad contrast to where we had just been. The crowd was now getting larger and larger. I noticed many poor women with us. They were chanting 'long live Egypt' and 'bread, freedom and social justice'. I never thought women like these would join the protest. Before the revolution when I used to go on demos where there were no more than 100 of us, these could have been the very same women who would spit on us and heap insults. The government had been very successful at spreading fear against anyone agitating against the regime. But today was different, today the barrier of fear came crashing down.

LOYALTY
by Sarah Helm

This play was first performed at Hampstead Theatre, London, on 14 July 2011.

Author and journalist, Sarah Helm, is married to Jonathan Powell, who was Prime Minister Tony Blair's Chief of Staff. Her play, *Loyalty*, chronicles their lives in the lead up to the Iraq invasion. Although Helm has changed her name to LAURA and her husband's name to Nick, other key players retain their identities, including Tony Blair. Helm calls it a 'fictionalised memoir'. Ultimately, LAURA questions the evidence that Blair's decisions are based upon, putting strain on her relationship with Nick.

LAURA

Faith. It had always bothered me when he used that word – ever since that Saturday in Hyde Park.

We'd been out for a family picnic and when we piled back in the car – parked opposite the Albert Hall – the bomb alarm went off so of course we all jumped out again, except Nick, that is. He was already on the car speakerphone, talking to Tony – who was in this car, driving down to Chequers – so Tony could hear our alarm in the background. He offered to ask his driver, Alan, what we should do. I remember noticing an Indian family walking towards us, exquisitely dressed for a wedding.

Feel under the wheel hubs for wires, was Alan's advice. So we both got down on our hands and knees, but I only felt cold slime. 'There's nothing,' says Nick to Tony. 'So what do we do now?'

Tony asked Alan. 'Alan says you'll probably be fine,' says Tony, still on the speaker. 'Yeah sure, of course, you'll be fine. Just try the ignition. Have faith Nick. OK? Speak later,' and he rang off.

So Nick moved his hand towards the ignition and as he did I pulled the children back down the pavement fast, then, seeing the wedding party, now level with the car, I suddenly screamed back: 'Stop! Did he say probably? Don't touch it. Jesus Christ! Stop!'

But I was too late. He'd turned the key.

The wedding family must have thought I was hysterical. Only later – when the bomb squad checked the engine – did they find it had been tampered with. 'We could have been scraping you off the Albert Hall,' they said.

ROADKILL
by Cora Bissett and Stef Smith

Roadkill *was conceived and directed by Cora Bissett and written by Stef Smith. The first performance was at the Tron in Glasgow in June 2010.*

Roadkill is a site-specific play, taking the audience on a journey by bus to a flat where the realities of human sex trafficking are revealed. MARTHA has 'bought' thirteen-year-old Mary from her family in Nigeria to be 'educated' in England. Mary soon learns that her 'education' consists of servicing men who visit their flat. She becomes pregnant and MARTHA wants her to have an abortion before Djall, 'The Boss', finds out about it. Mary refuses so MARTHA reveals her own story: she too is a victim of the African trafficking trade.

MARTHA

You have no idea what you are doing. If you leave right now you will kill your baby Mary. You will see it curl up and die in your own hands. You will see its beautiful brown eyes fill with tears. You will feel its tiny cold hands let go of yours. You have no idea. I watched my own sister die Mary! And she looked so like you. Maybe that's why I liked you. Eh! How foolish of me… Foluke was so much more beautiful. But she wasn't strong. She was not used to such force, such…frequency. By the end she couldn't even remember her own name. She sat and rocked and rocked, and screamed and screamed, hitting her head off the wall until it bled. Saliva just dripped down in a single string. No man would ever want her. So I had to do her men too. I had to do double. I had to keep her safe… I used to sing her songs like a child. It was only a matter of time before they would take her away. I went in to give her some chocolate – she smelt of shit and piss and she had torn out huge clumps of her hair…and she was praying. Those beautiful brown eyes. She fell asleep in my arms, I lay her down and I put a pillow over her face. I held her in my arms and she was peaceful Mary. Like a child. Like the sister I used to know, before I made this all happen… They had already taken so much from her at least she died beside me, she died with dignity.

ENTER THE SPOKESWOMAN, GENTLY

by Will Eno

from Oh, *the Humanity*
and other good intentions

This monologue was first performed as part of Oh, the
Humanity and other good intentions *at the Flea Theater,*
New York on 3 November 2007.

The SPOKESWOMAN for Country Air is speaking at a press
conference after one of the company's planes has crashed.
There are no survivors. She stands before a podium on which
are mounted several microphones.

SPOKESWOMAN

She enters.

Hello. First of all, let me just say that we are suffering with you families. Let me say, just, that we're suffering, we're staring at each other and up into the sky, like you, and that we have, while staring, tried to act. In a first very small step, we have as of tonight called off tomorrow's company picnic. I know that doesn't sound serious. We are canceling other events as well, because of the failure of the airplane. We don't know what we should do, honestly, or what we should say after doing it. But we do know the last thing anyone wants to see is us enjoying life, drinking too much and driving home drunk with someone from personnel, with a temporary tattoo and a sunburn. So, the picnic, of course, is off.

I have a father who died, incidentally. He taught me sports and going outside, picnic things. So I was just thinking about him. My father's gone, possibly as yours is, though mine died in a chair. He died sitting quietly, and not in a plane in flames, screaming downward at the speed of sound. His final resting place was an unraveling easy-chair in the living room. He was only human, and though it could have been, this was not listed as the cause of death. Countless nights beneath relatively fatherly men did nothing to lift the weight of that sad time. Excuse me, I'm sorry.

    Brief pause.

I don't know what it would be good for you to do. Try those things we all try.

A pause.

As for why, it is, as of tonight, undetermined. Who knows? Weather, an act of God or some handsome pilot's drunken error? Whatever it was, here we are. And we'll try to move forward, with time, taking hard comfort in the fact that, with or without us, time is moving forward, too.

A pause.

But, so, yes – it was flight 514, the night flight to Johnston, and there were, at this time, no survivors. We have been told so little so far. Gravity, we trust, was a factor. Did they know when it was still up that it was coming down? We hope not. We hope they felt secure on their airplane, as do we on our earth, and denied the fact of their coming doom, as do we ours. We hope they were enjoying the in-flight movie. Which was a Finnish film called *The Bleeding Parade*. I don't know if these small details are helpful.

…

I want to say – I'm the spokesperson, it's my job, and it's not easy – but I want to say to you: I understand, I think I understand. You waited and waited at the airport, you raced there in the first place, through unspeakable traffic, and the parking situation, and then you got to the proper gate and waited and they didn't come and didn't come and the monitor said DELAYED and I'm sure it was confusing, and then frustrating, and now just so sad. And can these things, can any sad things, ever even be compared? Is it insulting to you if I think they can? I'm sorry. My degree was in Hospitality

Management. I fell into this job through an acquaintance in the field.

A brief pause.

We're all going there, wherever, at different speeds, in different styles. I guess I am, as the spokesperson here, speaking to you, asking you to look around. Look at your hands. They used to be so tiny. Now they're not, and they're old. There are lines in our faces around our eyes from years of just laughing and using the wrong soap. The body is its own disaster area. The human face is a call for help. *Help, We need help, We are in flames, Port engine out, No radio. Landing gear is mangled, Radar is blank, Please foam the runway, We are coming in, coming home and down, and so shall you all.*

PART FOUR: FORTIES PLUS

THIS OTHER CITY
by Daragh Carville

This Other City was first performed in a production by Tinderbox Theatre Company at the Baby Grand Opera House, Belfast, on 30 April 2009.

GEMMA is a stylish 40 and runs a beauty business in Belfast. She is married to Patrick and mother to fifteen-year-old Orla. However, her world is turned upside down when she discovers Patrick's secret: he likes having sex with anonymous Eastern European prostitutes. The following scene is set in a counsellor's office, where GEMMA and Patrick are (supposedly) trying to save their marriage.

GEMMA

I know what I'm supposed to do. I mean, if it was somebody else, a friend of mine, a client, I know what I'd tell them to do. Chuck him out on his ear. Rip his lying, cheating throat out. Tear his bollocks off, all that. I'd be all for it. But it isn't someone else, it's me, and I have no frigging idea what to do. I don't have clue one. How to. Proceed.

And that's why I'm here.

…

Because I still have to go out there. Out into the world. Like – the opening of the new branch. I mean, I couldn't just decide to. Hide myself away. I have a business to run. And.

Orla laughs at this but. There are certain expectations.

So I went. Put my smiling public face on. As if it was all just, business as usual. And stood there and. Did my speech, welcoming everyone. Friends and clients. And my dad. And press and photographs. And afterwards, everyone asking, is Patrick here, how's Patrick. Chris and Eleanor and. And I just want to scream and. Do you know what he did, do you know what he is, do you know what he really.

But no. I smile and I say he's fine, he's doing great but sure you know how busy he is, you know what he's like. He wishes he could be here but. He sends his love. And big kisses and.

Watching myself, all the time. So I don't drink too much or. Give anything away. Do something stupid. Watching myself. The teller of lies. The keeper of secrets.

MOTHERLAND
by Steve Gilroy

This play was first performed at Live Theatre, Newcastle-upon-Tyne on 29 November 2007.

Motherland interweaves verbatim interviews with women who have been affected by the recent conflicts in Iraq and Afghanistan. JANICE is in her forties from Sunderland. Her son, Michael, was killed in Basra. Here's how she heard the news.

JANICE

On Sunday em... I got a phone call. It was about a couple of minutes after twelve. It said: 'Jan put your telly on Channel 24'. 'En up on the top 'British soldier killed the rest were injured, one critical'.

So then it was like palpitations, I ran put the computer on. Logged on. Cos you get the crest up of the badge and you click into the badge. Then me husband says: 'There's two women comin' to your door'. I went: 'Two women?'

I thought well it's Sunday. And at that split... [second] I just lost all recognition of who I was, what day it was. Didn't know nothing, d'y'know what I mean? Just didn't know nothing. And she just kept on saying: 'Are you Janice Murray? Are you Janice Murr...?' Well I took off up the stairs. I think I was going for me coat and me shoes, I think that's what I was doing, but I don't know, and then I come back down and she says: 'Are you...?' and I says: 'Who are you?' Cos I never like...but it's like...who are they? What do they want?

(Points to TV.) And I'm like: 'Have you seen that?' And she just looked. And I said: 'I'll be with you in two' cos I could not think what the hell was going on, but I said: 'Somebody's really going to have a nasty, nasty shock today'. And she says: 'I'm here to tell you...that it's your son', and I'm like: 'Oh my God'.

THE MEANING OF WAITING
by *Victoria Brittain*

This play was first produced as Waiting *in association with
Metta Theatre Company at the Purcell Room at the Southbank
Centre, London, on 12 March 2010. The production text of*
Waiting *was a modified version of the original* The Meaning of
Waiting *and was communicated through speech and song.*

Victoria Brittain has used verbatim text from interviews with
women whose husbands have been 'detained' as terrorist
suspects. They come from a variety of places (Palestine,
Senegal, Jordan, Libya as well as England) but they are united
by the terrifying wait for their men. SABAH is a Palestinian
from Jordan, who moved to Pakistan with her husband. The
couple fled to England as refugees where SABAH's husband
was taken by the Americans to Guantanamo. Although he was
cleared of his charges, SABAH is still waiting for him at the
end of the play. She has calculated his incarceration at 2,800
days. A final voiceover tells the audience that he was returned
to Britain in 2007.

SABAH

One time my solicitor brought me a report about Guantanamo from the Tipton people. It was so bad what they said about my husband's health, and about what happen inside there. What Americans do to men... I cant bear it, but I cant show anything in front of the children. I go to sit in the park where the children run and don't see my face. I cant tell my mother, I don't want her to worry, though sometimes she hears from my voice.

I have to be so careful for everyone, the children, my Mum, my husband, his family. Never say a negative word, never show what I feel.

I tell him in my letters, don't worry, the children are good, they do well in school, the littlest ones are funny, I'm fine. Your wife is still patient, you'll be strong too. I want to push him, be strong, Allah will help you with this test.

Inside I'm crying. I tell myself, don't be sad, it's stupid, you have only one life, don't throw it away in sadness.

I can only pray. I know Allah is doing this test for me, for him, for a reason.

I read Koran, and read, and pray for strength.

One time the lawyers arranged permission so I could speak to my husband on the telephone after all these years..... There no words for the emotion when I heard his voice.....

...

Afterwards I went home to the children and I told them, Dad is fine, don't worry, he'll come soon, he kisses you all, he knows you are good children. You'll see him soon.

Then in the mosque for Eid, people kept coming to me and hugging me, saying how good for the telephone call with your husband. They were kind and happy for me…

But no one knows except Allah what is happening for me, what is in my heart.

SABBAT
by Richard Shannon

Sabbat *was first performed at The Dukes in Lancaster on 29 January 2009. It was revived in 2012 commemorating the 400ᵗʰ anniversary of one of the most infamous witch hunts in British history.*

Four hundred years ago the 'Pendle Witches' were condemned to death at Lancaster Castle. Sabbat commemorates their story. When a young girl curses a peddler and he is struck dumb and lame, she is arrested for witchcraft. At her interrogation, she tells of a coven where 'murders' were planned. One of the women she names is ALICE NUTTER, a wealthy widow in her 40s. ALICE was midwife to the Prosecutor's wife but the child was stillborn. Grief-stricken, the Prosecutor adds this to her list of 'crimes'. In this scene, the Prosecutor tries to provoke a confession from ALICE but she stands her ground. Not long after ALICE is hanged.

ALICE

I am no witch.

You may ask and ask again 'til doomsday, but I will not change my answers.

…

I care not what you do to me.

Save your pity for the women you condemn, whose only crime is poverty.

   Beat.

But in truth, I know there is no pity in you.

Your mind is set on death.

   Beat.

You would line every road in Lancaster with gibbets.

For every small offence upon the road or in the home – shall the women swing? Girls and old maids, mothers and grandmothers, sons and daughters, curious men and the priests of Rome. We will hang in rows like sacks. Our hair shall be home to birds and mice and our empty eyes shall weep tears of blood.

And soon, in summer's heat our stench will make you stop your nose. The wind will scream his music through our ribs and you will see the pattern of our bodies washed clean by rain.

Then we will be cut down and lie together in a stack without a prayer.

Beat.

Do you think that you can silence all your fears and stifle all your disappointments by killing us? By taking our poor flesh and carving out a shrine to your misery?

You prick our skin, and flame our heads – hair burnt out black to stubble. You strip us naked in the market squares to search out the Devil's mark and never, never once look to inward sores – to sins that lie so heavy on your heart.

…

There are no more words. I will not confess. I am innocent.

THE HERETIC
by Richard Bean

The Heretic was first performed at The Royal Court Jerwood Theatre, London, on 4 February 2011.

DR DIANE CASSELL is a Paleogeophysics and Geodynamics lecturer in her 40s. She doesn't agree with commonly held views on the causes of climate change, which she spoke about in a television interview without permission from the university. Her line manager and ex-lover, Geoff, is in the process of sacking her along with Catherine the Human Resources Officer.

DIANE

What happened to the beautiful boy I fell in love with in a tent overlooking Isafjord?

…

He began his seduction by teaching me how to gut a cod. Stick your thumb and index finger in the fish's eyes, the eyes will pop out, but, hell's bells, don't cry for me Argentina, the fish is dead. Find the gateway of bones below the gills and run the knife quickly south dragging the guts out with your trailing thumb. Wash the fish in the fjord, triple wrap in foil and place in the embers. Whilst it's cooking, create a map-sized Rizla, spread evenly with tobacco from two broken cigarettes, and dress with the crumblings from a lump of Lebanese. Lick the Rizla along its length, and look the girl in the eye. She will blush. Tell her your heroes. Robert Johnson – King of the Delta Blues singers, Charles II, Henry Miller, Rosa Parks – why Rosa Parks and not Martin Luther King? Because her motivation was pure, not political. She was on a bus, tired, and she wanted to sit down. Your enemies were hilarious. Mother Teresa of Calcutta – pure evil?! Gandhi – a cretin!? The clergy of all religions. On science, brilliant, but frightened. The enlightenment project would never be secure because of the ubiquitous human need to be crushed under the wheels of the supernatural. And then a hand found its way under my jumper and cupped my left breast. I welcomed it. I was in love. That was a tutorial, Kevin. Not cost effective obviously, but inspirational. What happened to you? *(Beat.)* I've finished. You can sack me now.

DON JUAN COMES BACK FROM THE WAR

by Odon von Horvath
in a new version by Duncan Macmillan

Don Juan Comes Back from the War *was first performed at the Theatre of Courage, Vienna, in 1952. Duncan Macmillan's version was first performed at the Finborough Theatre, London on 28 February 2012.*

When Don Juan returns from the war he makes up for lost time with significant debauchery. However, he is no longer the man he once was and soon finds himself hospitalised. A woman, distraught over her daughter's death in an asylum for which she blames Don Juan, tries to stab him. He escapes from the hospital to try and find her but mistakenly arrives on the doorstep of the MOTHER and her young daughter. Don Juan had an affair with the MOTHER when she was a girl and, in this monologue, she describes to him how much pain his departure caused her.

MOTHER

look at you.

She drinks.

Stood in my kitchen

,

I'm just one of hundreds aren't I?

thousands maybe.

But to me, you're

,

He sits down near her. She smiles.

,

you were so handsome.

She touches his face.

Came along at just the wrong time.

Parents fighting.

Body changing.

Summer.

And you.

The whole universe.

Forbidden. A gentile.

Like staring into the sun.

I thought
this is life. This is living.

I was valued. Priceless.

The words you used. A rich man talking about love.

,

When you were gone it was a punch in the stomach.

Heard stories of you with other girls.
Friends. Sisters of friends. Mothers of friends.

I'd thought you were mine.

She smiles. She takes her hand away from his face. She drinks,
looks at the glass.

Tried to get that feeling back. With anybody.

Boys.

Passed around.
A dish rag.

Undeserving of real affection. Distrustful of it.

After three or four it was a pride thing.
This is what I am.
Ten. Twenty.

Thrown out of home.

Fifty. Sixty.

Hated every one of them.
Willing them to prove me wrong.

None did.

Not for years.

Then

got lucky. Her dad.

He was a good one.

Stuck around.

Dealt with my past.

My anger.

Listened.

I cried it all out and he held me. Dried my cheeks with his thumbs.

He'd lie awake grinding his teeth. Breathing through his nose.

He'd rip your throat out if he was here.

A WALK IN THE WOODS
by Lee Blessing

A Walk in the Woods *was first performed at Yale Repertory Theatre on 20 February 1987. A new version, changing one of the male characters to female (John to Joan) premiered at the Tricycle Theatre, London on 12 October 2011.*

Set in the Cold War, two arms negotiators try to navigate their way through a long-term stand-off. Andrey Botvinnik, 57, is the veteran Soviet negotiator: JOAN HONEYMAN, 45, is the American negotiator (originally from Wisconsin) and new to the job. Essentially, the play is a series of informal meetings between Botvinnik and HONEYMAN in the woods above Geneva, away from the negotiating table, where a strange friendship develops between them. The following scene shows how the futility of the negotiation is starting to get to JOAN.

JOAN

It was nothing. I threw a gum wrapper on the sidewalk. Really, there are more important things to talk about.

…

It was nothing. I threw this wrapper, and suddenly there was this very old man beside me, grabbing me. I thought he was a lunatic – he was yelling at me in German. Why did he yell at me in German? Do I dress like a German? He was trying to make me stop. I speeded up – I didn't know who he was.

…

He yelled at me louder – in French this time. I stopped and stared at him. I didn't say anything, I just stared. He kept right on yelling, only he switched to Italian. This went on for a solid minute – like I was his bad child – *all* in Italian. Finally I broke in. I said, 'I don't speak Italian,' and he went back to French.

…

So I yelled back at him: 'I don't speak French, German or Italian! I'm an American, damn it! What the hell do you want?! And he turned and pointed at my gum wrapper. And then I saw he was a cop. He was a Swiss policeman.

…

I didn't notice at first. He had his hat in his hand, and he was so…old, that I… But there he was, in uniform. He must've been going to his retirement party.

…

And he tried to drag me back to this gum wrapper. He literally tried to drag me. I said, 'Tell me what you want.' And he said, '*Aufheben!*' The paper. '*Aufheben!*'

…

I didn't pick it up.

…

Well, I didn't. I pulled my arm away. I wanted to say, 'Look – spend all day, every day, working to prevent the total destruction of every living thing on this planet. The whole planet. Even Switzerland. I'm trying to preserve the last few precious days of life you may have coming to you. But I can't do it if I'm not allowed to throw gum wrappers on the sidewalk. Do you understand? It's too much pressure! I can't worry about everything!'

…

No. I said, 'I'm a very important person.'

…

Then he tried to arrest me. He flashed his pitiful Swiss badge and put his hat on. By this time old people were stopping, looking at me and shaking their heads. As though the wrapper was a…dead infant or something. A couple of teenagers were standing there, laughing.

…

Anyway, he tried to grab me again, and I…I don't know why I did this, but I actually…pushed him.

…

I don't know why I did it.

…

…he didn't even fall over. But the others – the people around us – they gasped. They literally gasped. The old cop stared at me like I was insane.

…

So I quickly pulled out my identification and held it open and said, 'Diplomat.' And pointed to myself. And the cop just…shrank…from me. I took a step toward him and said, 'Diplomat' again, and he just kept backing away. And the whole crowd backed away. I kept saying, 'It's all right – I'm a diplomat,' but the circle of people got wider and wider and the cop turned and walked away from me as fast as he could. And everyone else did the same. Except the two teenagers. They just stared at me. Not like they expected me to do anything. Just…because I was the only thing left to look at. *(A beat.)* I've never behaved that way in public before.

…

I was not having a bad day! I was…I am turning into something here. Some kind of monster. Some kind of monster. Some kind of littering, old-man-pushing, diplomatic…monster. Some special, newly created kind of… *thing. (A beat. Quietly.)* What are we doing here?

PALACE OF THE END
by Judith Thompson

This play was first performed in London at the Arcola Theatre on 26 October 2010.

NEHRJAS is an Iraqi woman in her forties or early fifties. She was tortured, alongside of her children, in Saddam Hussein's Palace of the End. In this section of her monologue, NEHRJAS explains how her brother arrived home after being taken there.

NEHRJAS

One day they took my little brother. He was a silly boy, he liked to dance with girls and drink alcohol and wear expensive clothing and he was at the university. He was taken. We did not know where he was. We received a phone call in the morning. 'We are sending him home in a taxi.' We waited all day. The taxi arrived. The driver said Allah akh bar. 'There is a God' – because my brother was, Incredibly, still alive.

We rushed him into the house because if the neighbours saw they would shun us – they would be afraid of guilt by association. And he – he was so badly beaten we couldn't recognise his face, and he, he could see nothing. My other brother cried and my mother said, 'Don't cry! This is the way men learn to be men.' It seems harsh, but you have to understand the way we lived, and what it was to be a man. So, the monsters we lived in fear of were the Baath secret police, 'Jihaz Haneen.' If you can believe it, in English? The Instruments of Yearning. Can you explain that to me please? The torture jail was a fairytale castle, from long ago where the king had lived – we had not liked him either, he was Saudi but he was nothing compared to Saddam. The gardens were tended by a master gardener, a true genius of nature. And so the castle was called The Palace of Flowers. Until the Dark Age. When it became The Palace of the End.

'Qasr-al-Nihayah.' Iraq's own house of horrors; our children weren't afraid of fictional witches or monsters, those stories are only for peaceful places, our children had nightmares about the Palace of the End. 'O people of Iraq… By God,

I shall strip you like bark, I shall truss you like a bundle of twigs, I shall beat you like stray camels… By God, what I promise, I fulfil; what I purpose, accomplish; what I measure, I cut off.'

So said al-Hadjadj, the newly arrived governor of Iraq, in the year 694.

So said Saddam.

So said George Bush and Tony Blair.

And here we are. So.

HAND-ME-DOWNS

by James Graham

from *SIXTY-SIX BOOKS: 21ˢᵗ-Century Writers Speak to the King James Bible*

Sixty-Six Books: 21ˢᵗ-Century Writers Speak to the King James Bible *was first performed at the Bush Theatre in London on 10 October 2011. On 14 and 28 October, the sixty-six texts were performed back-to-back in an all-night vigil at the Bush. On 28 October they were performed complete at Westminster Abbey.*

Sixty-Six Books is a celebration of the 400th anniversary of the King James Version of the Bible. Sixty-six writers were commissioned to interpret a book from the KJV for the twenty-first century. They included playwrights, poets, novelists and songwriters differing in gender, age, ethnicity, sexual orientation and faith. *Hand-Me-Downs* is James Graham's response to '2 Timothy'. PAULINE is somewhere between her mid-forties and mid-fifties and runs a clothing swap internet business. Her daughter, Rachel, is a junkie and left home without a forwarding address. PAULINE shares her thoughts on Rachel with the audience.

PAULINE

She left, God, what are we on now, erm…

Why do people do that? Pause, pretend they're trying to think of something, even though they already know it in their head; I know exactly when she left, it was seven months and two days ago.

I don't know why I pretended I didn't, sorry.

Didn't think she could get better if she was…well 'here'.

I get emails. Used to be letters, people sent, didn't it? Although I suppose with this kind of thing, like Rachel, with letters there was always a danger of being found, what with the postmark and everything. All that palaver about catching a bus to a different town and posting it there. Exhausting.

But with an email she can send it from anywhere, and I'd have no idea.

So I suppose I'm grateful for that.

She always says three things.

She says that she's fine.

She says that she's sorry.

And she says she hopes I understand.

I know she's fine. She's strong, stronger than she – well, you know, apart from the obvious, but that can bring down anyone can't it, *has* brought down, bodybuilders, and…hasn't it. This 'affliction'. Or disease; meant to call it.

I know she's fine.

I know she's sorry.

And *of course*… I understand…

I didn't; didn't used to, that's why she says it, as her third thing. God I cringe now at some of the things I said to her, ignorant, just ignorant bloody…*things*, assumptions.

You think you know stuff, about stuff, don't you, but you don't know *anything*, it's just assumed. From magazines or soaps or the news.

But we weren't that kind of family, it wasn't in our, like DNA – whow, wait, no *(Slaps her hand.)* I've been told off about that, naughty. It *is* in our DNA, I mean it obviously *is*, isn't it, it must be in mine, passed down from me to her. This kind of…erm… (what was the word she?)…'disposition'. Chemicals in your brain or something, an imbalance, or something, making you more vulnerable to, like, this stuff. To addiction. And things. Apparently.

PUB QUIZ IS LIFE
by Richard Bean

Pub Quiz is Life was first performed at Hull Truck Theatre on
10 September 2009.

Lee (an ex-soldier), Bunny (his father and ex-dock worker),
Woody (a drug dealer) and Melissa (who works for a city
regeneration company) form a losing pub quiz team in Hull.
They all have their problems but their primary focus is on
beating a constantly winning team of teachers. MABEL runs
the pub quiz. She is in her fifties and described as 'busty, brash,
rather over-painted, like a ship's figurehead.' This monologue
occurs at the beginning of the play: MABEL introduces pub
quiz night to the players in her own inimitable style.

MABEL

It's Tuesday, at the White Horse. That can only mean one thing. Yesterday was Monday. Welcome to my pub quiz night adventure, an orgy, I wish, of trivia. A magical mystery tour without seatbelts down the highways and byways of the known universe. I'll be stopping the bus every two hours for a pee. My name's Mabel, and my quiz is much better than Master Mindyourownbusiness, cos Magnus Magnusson an't got much of a cleavage, and I mek up all me own questions using only me general knowledge, and the internet's wikipaedophilia. Any road, Magnus Magnusson's dead, so that's the end of that argument with a door. Anyone caught using a mobile phone will have their nuts crushed, they'll be stripped naked, and nailed to a sun bed and left outside Hammonds. If you need me to repeat a question, I have been known to repeat, then put your hand up, and I'll sort you out one at a time, as the actress said to the gathered synod. Round one, who played keyboards with the Hitler Youth Orchestra and the 1970s jazz fusion band Weather Report?

GROUPIE
by Arnold Wesker

Groupie *was commissioned by BBC Radio 4 and transmitted on 23 November 2001. The first stage performance was in Italian by the Gli Ipocriti company from Naples at the Festival di Todi on 21 July 2002.*

MATTY is 61 years old and finds herself drawn towards the famous painter Mark Gorman after reading his autobiography. She finds the courage to write to him (after discovering that he grew up in the same part of London's East End as herself) and soon there is an exchange of letters. However, when MATTY turns up on Mark's doorstep unannounced, she finds his living conditions unsavoury, his talent neglected, and his attitude hostile. Despite this MATTY perseveres and their relationship develops. In this monologue, MATTY shares with Mark early memories of her failed marriage.

MATTY

My husband asked me – what kind of a marriage do you want this to be? And I told him a story. One day, when I was about fifteen and fed up with too much piano practice, I started gazing out of the window. I used to do that for hours, thinking: every face is different. Amazing! Millions of faces in the world and apart from identical twins no two faces are the same.

And as I was looking out of the window I noticed a bird in the middle of the road. It was an owl. An owl in the middle of the road! Owls don't sit in the middle of the road I thought, perhaps it's hurt itself. I had to go outside and investigate.

It didn't look hurt so I tried to shoo it away. But would it move? Never. Fluttered its wings and stayed right where it was. Just then a small van drew up. From the Council. And out came this old councilman, and he said: *'She's sitting on a manhole. There must be something underneath.'* He couldn't shift the owl to find out, she kept snapping at him. So he drove to another manhole and worked his way underneath to this one. And do you know what he found? Her partner. Weak but still alive. She'd been keeping guard, attracting attention. How the one got into the hole and the other knew he was there is a mystery, but *that* I told him, is the kind of marriage I want.

BODIES UNFINISHED
by Lewis Hetherington

*This play was first performed by Grey Swan at the Brockley
Jack Studio Theatre on 14 July 2011.*

JOYCE is in her seventies and has just been moved into a care
home by her son, Alan. She isn't able to look after herself anymore
and neither can Alan (his life is in a mess). JOYCE is locked
away in her own world unable to communicate. Her monologues
are her inner voice reminiscing aloud. Here, we discover why
JOYCE became disconnected from Alan when he was a child.

JOYCE

We would go on holiday together
me, my man and Alan.
We'd go to the Isle of Lewis.

I liked Lewis.
Scraggy rocks everywhere.
It was like the moon I used to say and my man would
laugh at me.
But it was
so far from life on earth
it was the moon.

And that is where he died
my beautiful husband
One side, clutching at my hand was Alan,
I remember because that's the last time I ever touched him.
And on my other hand was my man
our hands slotted together just right
I thought nothing can hurt us.

Perhaps I didn't have those exact words clearly formed
in my head.
But it feels like I was thinking, nothing bad can happen
to us
when all of a sudden, there and then, his heart stopped.
And he sunk down
clumsy, fast and ugly
His body jerked
he made a noise like a crack in his throat
and he fell into the rocks.

I was so shocked I
I couldn't think I couldn't move
and I

he was dead.
His face was bloody and swollen
a cut tearing across his cheek
red raw hands lay at his side
cold and wet like his stone bed.

And I ran
ran and ran
couldn't look at either of them
left me son
and my dead lover
no goodbye
no final moment.

I went to the police of course
they put me in a room with a comfy sofa
and went to find my dead husband and my son.

They found my man.
Little Alan standing guard over his body
Little Alan watched and waited with his father
I'm jealous of him for that.

I remember, when they brought him back to me at the
station
I thought if I could have my man back and lose Alan I
would.
I would let Alan go.

They said that he just had such sudden and aggressive
heart attack that he was dead more or less instantly.
He was drained
and became a piece of rock
there was no saving him.

So that was that.

The Books

BLACKBERRY TROUT FACE
by Laurence Wilson

ISBN: 9781849432436

THE WOMAN BEFORE
by Roland
Schimmelpfennig / David
Tushingham

ISBN: 9781840025729

APPLES
by John Retallack

ISBN: 9781849430982

NIGHTBLIND
by Darja Stocker

from *Theatre Café:
Plays Two*

ISBN: 9781849430227

**BUD TAKE THE WHEEL, I
FEEL A SONG COMING ON**
by Clara Brennan

ISBN: 9781849430760

MUHAMMAD ALI AND ME
by Mojisola Adebayo

from *Mojisola Adebayo:
Plays One*

ISBN: 9781849430753

SENSE
by Anja Hilling

from *Theatre Café:
Plays Two*

ISBN: 9781849430227

PROTOZOA
by Kay Adshead

from *The Oikos Project*

ISBN: 9781849430050

SHRADDHA
by Natasha Langridge

ISBN: 9781840029659

**LOVE STEALS US FROM
LONELINESS**
by Gary Owen

ISBN: 9781849430548

DNA
by Dennis Kelly

ISBN: 9781840028409

SUZANNAH
by Jon Fosse

from *Jon Fosse: Plays Five*

ISBN: 9781849430746

OPEN HEART SURGERY
by Laura Lomas
from *Theatre Uncut*
ISBN: 9781849430630

PALACE OF THE END
by Judith Thompson
ISBN: 9781849430074

FANTA ORANGE
by Sally Woodcock
ISBN: 9781849431965

AFTER THE END
by Dennis Kelly
ISBN: 9781840025804

MUSWELL HILL
by Torben Betts
ISBN: 9781849431378

DEEP HEAT
by Robin Soans
ISBN: 9781849430906

MANY MOONS
by Alice Birch
ISBN: 9781849430777

BLUE HEART AFTERNOON
by Nigel Gearing
ISBN: 9781849431392

MOTHERLAND
by Steve Gilroy
ISBN: 9781840029482

LULLABIES OF BROADMOOR: THE MURDER CLUB
by Steve Hennessy
ISBN: 9781849431620

DEEP CUT
by Philip Ralph
ISBN: 9781840028744

BODIES UNFINISHED
by Lewis Hetherington
ISBN: 9781849431293

BELONGINGS
by Morgan Lloyd Malcolm
ISBN: 9781849432252

WE'RE GONNA MAKE YOU WHOLE
by Yasmine Van Wilt
ISBN: 9781849431316

DREYFUS INTIME
by George R. Whyte
from *The Dreyfus Affair: A Trilogy*
ISBN: 9781849430371

LOYALTY
by Sarah Helm
ISBN: 9781849432092

JOY AND TYRANNY
by Arnold Wesker
ISBN: 9781849431088

ROADKILL
by Cora Bissett/
Stef Smith
ISBN: 9781849431989

MARY MASSACRE
by Johnny McKnight
ISBN: 9781849431385

THIS OTHER CITY
by Daragh Carville
ISBN: 9781849430494

ORPHANS
by Dennis Kelly
ISBN: 9781840029437

MOTHERLAND
by Steve Gilroy
ISBN: 9781840029482

MIXED UP NORTH
by Robin Soans
ISBN: 9781840029604

THE MEANING OF WAITING
by Victoria Brittain
ISBN: 9781849430517

MY BEST FRIEND
by Tamsin Oglesby
ISBN: 9781849430609

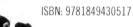

THE HERETIC
by Richard Bean
ISBN: 9781849431200

THE PROPHET
by Hassan Abdulrazzak
ISBN: 9781849434492

ENTER THE SPOKESWOMAN, SIDEWAYS
by Will Eno
from *Oh, the Humanity and other good intentions*
ISBN: 9781840028324

DON JUAN COMES BACK FROM THE WAR
by Odon von Horvath /
Duncan Macmillan

ISBN: 9781849432542

PUB QUIZ IS LIFE
by Richard Bean

ISBN: 9781840029598

A WALK IN THE WOODS
by Lee Blessing

ISBN: 9781849431811

GROUPIE
by Arnold Wesker

ISBN: 9781840029550

HAND-ME-DOWNS
by James Graham

from *Sixty-Six Books: 21st-Century Writers Speak to the King James Bible*

ISBN: 9781849432276

SABBAT
by Richard Shannon

ISBN: 9781849432467

All the above books can be ordered from www.oberonbooks.com

OTHER CATHERINE WEATE TITLES

Oberon Book of Modern Monologues for Men
9781840028256

Oberon Book of Modern Monologues for Men 2
9781849434362

Oberon Book of Modern Monologues for Women
9781840028263

Oberon Book of Modern Duologues
9781840028287

**Classic Voice: Working with Actors
on Vocal Style**
9781840028270

**Modern Voice: Working with Actors
on Contemporary Text**
9781849431712

WWW.OBERONBOOKS.COM

Follow us on www.twitter.com/@oberonbooks
& www.facebook.com/oberonbook